wôrd·crâft

ALEX FRANKEL

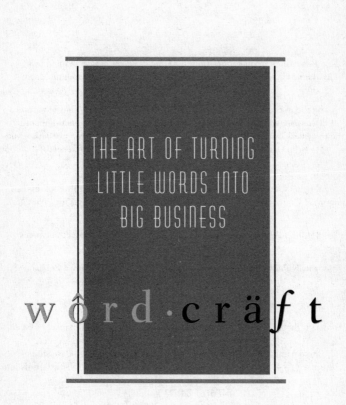

THE ART OF TURNING
LITTLE WORDS INTO
BIG BUSINESS

wôrd·cräft

Three Rivers Press – New York

Copyright © 2004 by Alex Frankel

All rights reserved. Published in the United States by Three Rivers Press, an
imprint of Crown Publishing Group, a division of Random House, Inc., New York
www.crownpublishing.com

THREE RIVERS PRESS and the Tugboat design are registered trademarks
of Random House, Inc.

Originally Published in hardcover in the United States by Crown Publishers, a
division of Random House, Inc., New York, in 2004.

Library of Congress Cataloging-in-Publication Data
Frankel, Alex.
Wordcraft: the art of turning little words into big business / Alex Frankel.—1st ed.
Includes bibliographical references.
1. Brand name products—Case studies.   2. Business names—Case studies.
3. Advertising.   4. Marketing.   5. Creative ability in business.   I. Title: Words into
big business.   II. Title.
HF6161.B4F73   2004
658.8'27—dc22   2003019670

ISBN 1-4000-5105-3

Printed in the United States of America

DESIGN BY ELINA D. NUDELMAN

2   4   6   8   10   9   7   5   3   1

First Paperback Edition

For my mother and father
and for
B. T. Nichols

Capitalist Graffiti, Global Tongue, Dispatches from the Language Industry, The Corporate Voice, Pieces of Information, Wordsmith, Adventuring into the New Branded Future, Fabricated Words, Writ Large, New Nouns, Word for Word, Whiteboard Graffiti, Quick Words, Buzz Words, The Corporate Voice, 26 Letters, Pieces of Information, Linguistic Landscape, The Ultimate Global Shorthand, **WORDCRAFT**, That Which Makes a Thing What It Is, Off the Whiteboard into the Lexicon, Word Factory, Idea Market, What You Call It, Venture X, The Shortest Story, Coining Names and Launching New Language, The Intangible Revolution, Corporate Poetry, The Fun Stuff, Adventures in the Corporate Language Industry, Wordscapes, Big-Ticket Nouns, The Spoken Words of Corporate America, Household Names, Utopian Turtletop, Figures of Speech, Global Graffiti, Whiteboard Magic, Brand Tourist, Idea Culture, New Language for a New World, Words That Wander, From Whiteboard to Billboard, Indelible Markers, Word Nerds, The Idea Speaks for Itself, Firing Up the InkJets, Elevator Pitch, Whiteboarding, Into the WordStream, Divergent Thinking, The Sloppy Process, Verbal Inventions, Naming Names, The Word Hunters

New words, of course, are no more produced by the folk than are new ballads: they are the inventions of concrete individuals, some of whom can be identified.

—H. L. Mencken, *The American Language*

AUTHOR'S NOTE

This book is a work of nonfiction. All sources and subjects are real people. In writing a book about the people who make up words and stories, it is a consistent challenge to separate true stories from those in which some party is "drinking the Kool-Aid," either telling or believing stories that others will buy into. Diligent pre-readers of this book were asked to note when they thought the author was casting aside his better judgment in the face of Kool-Aid. It should be noted that Kool-Aid is a synthetic fruit juice manufactured by Kraft Foods, of which 563 million gallons are consumed each year, and there are, at this printing, twenty-two flavors. Kool-Aid is also the shorthand for a way of thinking, a point to be made in the pages that follow.

CONTENTS

CONTENTS

w ô r d · c r ä f t

HUNTING

WORDS

1

When I arrived at nine in the morning, I found a low-ceilinged room that once had been a U.S. Navy vault. Its walls were covered with whiteboards and its center dominated by a large wooden table. I pulled up a chair and got out paper and pen. I joined a group that sat thinking and blurting out ideas, six of us trying to come up with a name for a new computer network. We hunkered around the table while a set of floor heaters crackled. It was my first day as a freelance namer, and we were making up a word.

Our group of six, including an actress, a poet, a computer programmer, and me, a business journalist, spent the day naming a computer network that would be used by small businesses. We looked no different from corporate workers casually dressed in loose-fitting blouses, button-down shirts, and khakis. At first our task seemed mundane, basic. But as our leader goaded us to think about this new word in different ways, through different angles and filters, the task assumed great depth and importance.

At the outset he asked us simply, "What does a computer network do?" The question hung in the air like a Zen koan . . . *What is the sound of one hand clapping?* By midday we recognized the almost tangible gravity and importance affixed to our naming project. We ran through dozens of exercises designed to tap the ideas we had in our heads, to get them out on paper, and to get us to keep things fresh, to avoid static thinking. The very idea of a new network twisted and morphed before us—seen at one moment as a light-rail system, then as a steel girder infrastructure, briefly as a bible. We tossed out words—*Ensemble, Copernicus, Socket, Tango, Chainlink.* We filled sheets of butcher paper with words penned in many hues, tore pictures from magazines, wrote advertising slogans, and watched television commercials about the company selling the network. The task was not so much to come up with one single winning word but to brainstorm hundreds of possibilities—to get *all* the ideas out. Someone else would sift through them later.

I went home that evening with a legal pad filled with scrawled, esoteric notes: *data river = information ecosystem, interfusing + Galapagos—>braindock!!, ear to the ground, life versus company, the network that moves mountains.* And even a few hastily jotted haikus: *Rising from the dust / An unstoppable success / A chorus of one* and *The fabric of work / Gliding effortlessly fast / Zigging and zagging.*

Naming the network gave me a sudden glimpse into another world. It seemed strange and futuristic, weird that we were being paid $300 a day to create a noun—a person, a place, or (in this case) a *thing.* As I began to look around with a more critical eye over the next few months, I saw a full-fledged language industry whose work was synthesizing words. And I met an array of people creating new words or reassigning existing ones to drive commerce forward by getting people to use certain words and change people's behavior. Like so many other things in our prepackaged world, it seemed, words, too, were being turned out with factory-like efficiency, crafted to fit into our vocabularies.

But in the beginning, a word is just a word. The word might be scribbled in dry-erase marker on a whiteboard (like so many that day), uttered by an executive during a corporate brainstorm meeting, dreamed up by a naming consultant in the shower, or spewed out of a computer. It might be an existing word or a brand-new combination of characters. It might have specific connotations for a listener, or it might be totally foreign. At its outset, a brand name is just a string of letters without much meaning in relation to the product to which it is attached. But then it moves from being a word to being a name. And, finally, emerging like a butterfly into the world, it becomes a full-fledged *brand* name.

Sometimes the word succeeds beyond the wildest dreams of its creators, like a virus sent into the world to infect common speech. This is a successful brand launch. The created word is loaded with meaning, and the public responds well to that meaning, embraces it, becomes loyal to it, makes it a "household" name. Names can be emotional, contentious, controversial, valuable, dramatic, poetic, powerful, manipulative, human, cultural, international, invisible, pervasive, and ubiquitous.

As a culture, we have become a world of speed-readers, able to scan a newspaper article from the headline and understand an advertisement by just glancing at it. A name, if it is constructed right, plays into this scheme, so that its intended audience will grasp it immediately and implicitly. Jean-Marie Dru, in his seminal business text *Disruption,* puts forth the notion that communication is no longer a product *attribute* but an integral *component* of a product. In other words, the product *is* the message.

For most humans, the act of learning language and new words is a constant, ongoing process, although it is most pronounced during the first two decades of life. People generally start talking at eighteen months of age. At age two, most babies know fifty words. By the age of three, this number surges to around one thousand. By six, the average child knows thirteen thousand words; at eighteen, around sixty thousand. This means that most of us learn an average of ten new words each day from our first birthday on—the equivalent of a new word every two hours of waking life. And increasingly these words are brand names.

The modern marketplace teems with brand names—with a corn chip called *Doritos Cooler Ranch,* a car called *Nissan Maxima,* a beer called *Moosehead,* ready-to-eat frozen meals called *Lean Cuisine,* a food processor called *Cuisinart,* an airline called *Virgin Atlantic,* and a pain pill called *Tylenol* (derived from the chemical name for acetaminophen, N-acetyl-p-aminophenol). Each name, through heavy advertising, means something to every consumer. But how far, really, are these words from those I had scribbled in the meeting I attended . . . words like *braindock* and *interfusing* that seem totally meaningless?

By the time I had become a creator of new brand names, I was well aware that we live in a world filled with them, that brand names are a part of the soundtracks of our lives—some by chance, some on purpose—and that words owned by corporations have become core components of our modern language, if not a new language entirely, seeping into vernacular speech. Instead of drinking a cup of coffee, increasingly we "get *Starbucks.*" We "do the *StairMaster.*" We *fedex* packages, take an *Advil,* and apply *ChapStick.* These brand names are synecdoches—they represent larger things. By supplying meaning to consumers, brand names assume great worth in the marketplace. As adman Claude Hopkins writes, the best names "are almost complete advertisements in themselves."

Slowly but surely the many words created and trademarked by corporations have come to resemble a new language unto themselves—a sort of pan-human language for a globalized world. The act of creating and trademarking words almost ensures that big-time brand names will become part of a new brandspeak, or what Stanford linguist Geoffrey Nunberg has called a "lingua branda."

Colors of paint are no longer just reds, yellows, and blues but thousand of variations on the primary colors: Equator Glow (yellow), Yacht Harbor (blue), Evening Symphony (dark blue), Juicy Fig (brown). Ralph Lauren Paint has some of the most interesting names in the business: Farmer's Jacket (blue), Summer Espadrille (yellow), Morning Surf (blue), Pacific Sarong (green), Locker Room (black), and Yorkshire Hound (orange).

Great companies no longer prosper solely from the efficient production of goods but also from the ubiquity of their brand names, from the prevalence of their "concepts." In a book critical of what he calls "the new network economy," writer Jeremy Rifkin identifies the switch: "What is really being bought and sold [is] ideas and images. The physical embodiment of these ideas and images becomes increasingly secondary to the economic process. If the industrial marketplace was characterized by the exchange of things, the network economy is characterized by the access to concepts, carried inside physical forms." The ease with which consumers associate brand names with positive attributes now directly affects a company's market share. We live in the information age, and anything sold must become part of the data stream. The naming firms I happened upon, and later worked for, have the interesting job of creating and inserting verbal or text messages into this flood of data—they are coiners of words, information-age neologists.

Among the many players in the communications industry— advertising agencies, public relations firms, crisis management groups, and brand strategists—as a reporter I was attracted to the small naming firms. The field is filled with language crafters, makers of meaning who look at language in a clinical fashion, and who craft new words and appropriate existing words for new uses.

Discovering this group of namers was like finding the group of workers most emblematic of the new state of things, manipulators of the new postindustrial economy. The names that succeed seem to penetrate human interactions transparently. Others fail. I wanted to know how and why this happens.

As I studied it, I came to realize that the language of business has a mature grammar filled with brand names, multifaceted ideas, and more in-depth and far-reaching stories. Names, ideas, and stories are all, to a certain extent, figures of speech that can move the behavior of clients, customers, and employees—and, most important, make money. Language in the marketplace shapes how people act.

Most firms in this line of work go unnoticed, although their work ranges far and has great impact. They work in the background, crafting prose in clever ways for each client to put its own name on. It is a creative field, with little consensus on common practices. The best firms are those with an abiding interest in promoting effective language. Rather than championing buzzwords and jargon, these firms focus on understanding the landscape of commerce and how best to work within a world where intellectual property trumps physical property. Workers in the language industry apply themselves toward the fine art of understanding human nature so they may best place their concepts within an evolving material culture. The task of creating a new name—of taking a word or making up a word that can be smoothly inserted into the marketplace and into the vocabularies of consumers—is harder than it sounds. It's a lot easier to hand over an assignment to a specialized consultant who does nothing but name.

Hunting Words

Scholars credit William Shakespeare with coining some 1,500 words (including *lackluster, bandit,* and *watchdog*). But namers produce neither poetry nor high art; they create words that make money. How namers work is strange, but their output is also a strange commodity, as far from a product of the industrial age as you are likely to find. An odorless, shapeless, product-less product that still can be owned. A product that can be planted in a million virtual fields and harvested, growing and spreading as it shapes consciousness wherever it travels.

I decided to hunt down some of the more successful words, to track them from where I found them in the marketplace back to their points of origin. I sought to pluck them up and examine them and identify the unique features of each. I wanted to write their biographies. I decided to embark on a modern voyage of etymology.

Like an adventurer of old, bent on tracking words through space and time, I followed a handful of words to their birthplaces, to the latter-day factories that shaped and cut them from the whole cloth of the English language. If they all swam together now in a sea of data, a global ocean of colliding bits, each had to have had a point of entry—those points of embarkation were my destinations, their creators were my sources. Each word, I knew, had been fashioned by some group or some person somewhere. Some of the words I traced came from a handful of firms that led the field of language creators, who develop single words and all-encompassing lexicons. And some people guarded their tales more than others. Unlike natural or organically created words, the ones I stalked were synthetic bits of language, and some sought to parallel and imitate "real words" more than others.

For my yearlong adventure I chose five words: *BlackBerry, Ac-*

centure, Viagra, Porsche Cayenne, and *IBM e-business.* Each has its own story to tell about the new synthetic corporate language. BlackBerry is that rare word that helped its product succeed in ways it otherwise might not have. Accenture is as synthetic as they come, a test-tube concoction—wholly created from nothing. Viagra, in three years, penetrated that esteemed repository of language, the *Oxford English Dictionary.* The Porsche Cayenne, on the cusp of its own release into the world when I encountered it, remained a wild card. And e-business, I found, was a borrowed word that IBM never owned. As a group, these words came from a variety of places—the technology, consulting, pharmaceutical, and automotive industries. They were a representative batch of words that would allow me to gain an overview of naming things today.

Not coincidentally perhaps, many of the stories I found are about products made for communicating. The named things I found most interesting include personal devices for sharing text messages, consulting firms that help get messages across, and technology firms that build and run vast communication networks. For talking, sending email, sharing the bits and bytes that make up our current age, that make money and keep people employed. We live in an age of communications infrastructure, where much attention and energy are focused on the mere act of communicating—programming telephones, downloading information, checking voice mail, email, video-on-demand.

The stories in this book, whether about the communications firms or the products and services for which they have crafted language, show that the best words meet a need that a target audience has—not an artificial or manufactured need but a real one. Words, especially well-crafted words, change people's behavior. It is important to note that the pieces of language shown in the pages ahead, whether simple brand names or stories, were backed up by strong products and services. The most successful launches of language have been those that let their target audiences become a part of a narrative. The companies that combine strong products with the idea of integrating customer opinions and needs have, by and large, found success.

Porsche and *SUV* are two words that individually pack a lot of meaning. Putting the two together could spell disaster. Starting in the summer of 2002, Porsche rolled out a new SUV that it chose to call *Cayenne*. In naming the vehicle, Porsche studied its target audience, hoping to put itself in the driver's seat. Its message, after a long silence, became, "We know that you may think this new car, this Third Porsche, will dilute the Porsche brand, but just wait and see." Porsche needed to refocus the idea of the SUV, the backwoods image conveyed by *Sierra* and *Yukon*. Would *Cayenne* encompass not only a new SUV image but also Porsche's craftsmanship, speed, and myth?

In the first section of the book, on the creation of names, I look at people who craft single words intended to become brand names. I stop off at Lexicon Branding, the word fabrication factory where I first gained a glimpse into this hidden world. In this chapter on creating one single word, I show how the right word can do wonders for a product and the company selling that product. Lexicon successfully takes the pulse of consumer sentiment and matches a word to the feeling, moving bits of information by knowing just the right word consumers will respond to, long before those consumers even know what they want.

Lexicon had churned out dozens of brand names—household words like *Pentium* and *PowerBook*—when a small underdog Canadian technology company came calling in need of a good name. It was the kind of project that Lexicon's founder, David Placek, excels at—taking a piece of cutting-edge machinery and slapping on an equally forward-thinking name. RIM, the maker of what Placek and his staff came to call *BlackBerry,* already had competition from well-known players in the handheld computer and wireless telecommunications market, players like Palm Computing whose messages the public knew well. *BlackBerry,* an appropriate and original name, has blossomed into a brand. Without its name, the device and the company that manufactures it would not have moved as far, as fast.

By the time I turned my attention to *Accenture,* the word was everywhere—it was the centerpiece of a $175 million marketing campaign. Apparently the word was sent in to corporate headquarters by one of more than two thousand consultants at the company participating in an internal match. The word interested me mainly because it had been born by court order. Andersen Consulting and Arthur Andersen were happily united as sister companies until differences pushed them so far apart that a legal showdown forced Andersen Consulting to drop its name. An entire company had to change its signs and business cards and, more important, see itself as something new—and to convince clients of its credibility. I was curious how a large, old company chose a new name and how it affected the people who worked there. I wanted to know what it did to a group of people to remove a historic name they were all a part of. And why, I wanted to know, *Accenture*? In this chapter I explore the legal challenges and hurdles that just about any big-ticket noun faces in the marketplace. *Accenture,* a name created by an Andersen employee, shows the triumph of a new kind of name—the synthetic, just-add-water (and a lot of advertising dollars), umbrella name. As a language tool, it had a job to do, and when engaged in the marketplace, the word worked.

In the second part of the book I look into how the most powerful words grow into *ideas* with the power to sway behavior. Once a word like *FedEx* (or even *BlackBerry*) transforms into an idea, it has gained a toehold on the consumer psyche. An idea is a name with some extra value, some added connotation that makes the word more valuable to its owners. Ideally, the creator of a new word takes into consideration how the new word will move and travel, and how it will spread through people's vocabulary and gain a certain level of "talk value." But there are no tried-and-true rules for how to send words out.

At Wood Worldwide, the birthplace of such well-known pharmaceutical drug names as *Paxil* and *Prilosec*, creative director R. John Fidelino told me that a well-crafted name for a new drug must be an instant *idea*. Few people missed out on the 1998 launch of *Viagra*—the word, if not the pill itself, was suddenly everywhere. And this was not a huge surprise to the people behind the launch. Because of the subject matter, a stigmatized physical condition known as impotence, older marketing wisdom dictated a discreet name. But by bringing the drug and the carefully renamed disease into conversation, Pfizer got the word out at NASCAR speed. Soon other names would invade Viagra's territory and carve up its market share in advance of its sale as a generic drug, but Viagra owned its given window of time. A coined word, Viagra came to serve as an idea and a tool that people were ready and willing to use in speech.

I also found cases where language—names and ideas—were rolled into corporate stories. Those corporate stories—the good ones, anyway—are often created by firms in full command of how words alter and affect perceptions, so that the full power of particular words can have a lasting impact. Tracking down Keith Yamashita was no easy feat—there was no direct line from him to any of his work. But when I found him and talked to him, I discovered that he had had a hand not only in IBM's wide-reaching language efforts but also in efforts at IBM's competitors Hewlett-Packard and Apple Computer. In the last section of the book,

I look at the development of corporate stories, how these all-encompassing narratives are crafted and disseminated, and how they work to change behavior. In chapter 10, I look specifically at how IBM (with help from Yamashita's under-the-radar consulting firm) created its *e-business* story. This chapter shows that some firms craft entire stories, incorporating both names and ideas. It also looks at the "communications industry" and how companies like Apple have profited by concentrating so closely on words and language. IBM's *e-business* was a bigger story than just one word, and it worked because the story allowed IBM to recontextualize, rightly, where the whole Internet was headed. It made IBM relevant to itself *and* to consumers who were unsure what the digital future held.

These words, once constructed and released, must hold their own. They'll get sucked into all sorts of weather systems, some sunny, some stormy. Some will be anti-corporate, some pro-corporate, some philanthropic. They could be used in art, or as art. A lot will happen to them—some of which can be controlled, some of which cannot. People who come up with these words really can't rely on a simple formula; one success almost guarantees that a similar word won't succeed. Once you create Pentium or Power-Book and it owns a part of the market, you can't go there again.

Five little words: *BlackBerry, Accenture, Viagra, Cayenne, e-business*. Two of the words are appropriated (*BlackBerry* and *Cayenne*); two are completely made up (*Viagra* and *Accenture*); and one (*e-business*) is a composite word made of a word and a letter that already exist. As it happens, the two that were made up were advertised with abandon. *BlackBerry* seeped more slowly into the public consciousness before getting an advertising push. *Cayenne* was surrounded with a good deal of advertising that sought to marry the name with that of Porsche. IBM's *e-business* also was shipped out to the world in a dozen ways, heavily wrapped inside other messages and images. These five words are the characters in this book.

Naming Names

All names start in the same place: inside someone's brain, the brain of someone like Andrea Carla Michaels. Andrea Michaels was my own introduction into the world of naming. I met her randomly and unexpectedly while out with my friend Jessie for a Sunday-afternoon walk around San Francisco's North Beach. Meeting her was one of those chance encounters in life that sends one down an unexpected road with no return. Jessie smiled as I snapped a photograph on an ancient Polaroid Land Camera. Andrea, a slim and attractive woman of forty, walked by and took an interest in the camera. The three of us sat down and had a cup of coffee at an outdoor café.

Andrea was a namer. She had just been interviewed by Bob Garfield on National Public Radio about her profession, and I'd heard the broadcast while driving. I hadn't listened carefully to the radio story, but when she told Jessie and me how she made a living, I recalled bits and pieces. On the radio she described things she had named—an airline (Vanguard), a video dating service (Tango), a European popcorn product (Pop-A-Razzi), and an inflatable furniture company (Furnishair, Inc.).

She worked independently, she told us, but also for a number of these so-called naming firms that depended on people like her to supply initial fodder, starting points for naming projects. She had played a role in naming Monsanto's parasite-proof potato, the NewLeaf Potato, for one such firm. She was one of a handful of word creators, a sort of elite force of creative people who regularly supplied raw material to the firms that hired her—in the shape of words and ideas—for the wide-reaching brainstorming sessions and creative phases of name creation. "Naming is like songwriting, or haiku, but it's even more tightly constrained," another namer later explained. "It's creativity under constraint. You have to evoke shades of meaning in small words."

Andrea shared some of her story with us that first afternoon, enough to paint a picture of a typical corporate namer, if there could be such a thing. I was initially intrigued for selfish reasons when I met Andrea—I did not necessarily want to model my life after hers, but it occurred to me that as a recent college graduate with a literature degree, an ability to free-associate on command, and an interest in words, I had at least part of the skill set that would make me a good namer. It sounded like a fun way to spend one's time.

I came to view Andrea as a sort of foot soldier in a linguistic war being waged by corporate America where good, novel, inventive, and fresh ideas substitute for ammunition. When she walked into a naming firm and presented her credentials—Harvard education, knowledge of Greek, Italian, and French, obsession with Scrabble, keen observer of pop culture, hobby of writing crossword puzzles, slightly off-center worldview, addiction to trivia, and regular participation on game shows—they were likely to throw some work at her.

Andrea is a humor writer. Like a lot of the creatives I met, she's an artist with a set of knowledge that is useful in the corporate world. Some of the best new brand names emerge from this intersection of creative ideas and business strategy. The creative people who can best combine their skills with an understanding of the business landscape often supply the best answers. But they are a rare breed and come from a range of unpredictable disciplines. Summoned to boardrooms, these people often connect corporations to the rest of the world by shedding light on their products and philosophy and also by making lumbering giants seem nimble and relevant to average consumers.

Although Andrea has changed her look many times, I like to think of her with her hair worn in bleached spikes—hip with a somewhat timeless appearance. She could almost be a character in a Mad Max movie, a strong-willed and street-smart chick riding alongside Mel Gibson in a postapocalyptic world. She's reminiscent of the rock musician Ani DiFranco, a mature, sexy punk with quick-witted intellect. Andrea is neither a slick consultant nor a branding professional. Her employers would not want to parade her before a client, for fear of what candid remarks she might let slip. She's a loose cannon. But she can create and channel her verbal smarts in many directions, and she gets the job done.

Her résumé, which she submitted to me a couple of years after I first met her (when I myself was in the process of hiring her to help name something), is surprisingly fun to read. It's a long list of jobs that, as a group, are far-from-standard ways to make a living. She's peppered her professional career with outlandish pursuits, things that just plain did not exist twenty years ago. And you won't find everything she's done on her résumé. You won't see that she created a crossword puzzle for the *New York Times* in which she managed to sneakily spell out her name across the center. (The subject of her crossword was earthquakes; 39 across was *San Andreas Fault*.) She told me the crossword she produced was the best thing she did in 2000: "It's the puzzle of all puzzles." She spent months preparing the crossword and was paid seventy-five dollars by the *Times*. She recognizes that she does a lot of things that people would do for free. "If you love to do something, people might take advantage of that," she told me. Andrea found her way to naming because it provided a steady flow of work that combined an affinity for vocabulary words with a solid paycheck.

Andrea's love of words runs deep. When she was eight years old, she announced to her family that she wanted to change her name. Her father repeatedly talked her out of it and resorted to hiding her birth certificate. Eventually, when she was a stand-up comic in Los Angeles, she brainstormed some possibilities for her stage name (Maxfield and MaxMichaels were shortlist contenders). She then dropped her surname, Eisenberg, and started calling herself Andrea Carla Michaels. This first foray into naming was meant to give her a name that was Jewish-sounding enough so she didn't feel as if she were trying to change her identity. "My name sounded silly to me, so I changed it," she says. She was aware of how powerful names can be, how a word can help sell something. She also knew how important it is for the client to connect with the name—Michael is her dad's first name.

To Andrea, naming is just an extension of her game-playing, and her love of games parallels her infatuation with words. She's done just about all one can do to profit from a sheer love of words—not of writing or grammar but of just unadulterated words. She lets her brain get rented out and downloaded in the process of delivering ideas to clients. "Of course," Andrea tells me, "there's a direct relationship between my naming myself, my love of words, my love of Scrabble, being a comic-slash-writer, loving travel and therefore languages . . . and being a namer." Words are the protagonists in her personal Information Age drama.

Andrea has been on virtually every major game show at least once. Game shows and naming projects are more similar than they appear—quick engagements that test one's fast-reflex smarts. In July 1988, Andrea reached a personal milestone when she was selected as a contestant on *Jeopardy* after several qualifying rounds. The thrill of *Jeopardy*, she says, is in summoning an answer out of the air. "It's a question of retrieval—I'm pulling something out I learned in third grade. It's all these pieces of the puzzle coming together. It's synchronicity. It means making connections between words and people." But she flamed out. She lost to a military captain who appeared on the show in full uniform, nailed a final question on the Civil War, and set the all-time single-day *Jeopardy* prize record.

In 1991, Andrea appeared on *Wheel of Fortune,* where she sought to right all the wrongs of *Jeopardy*—it is a straight word game, after all. Originally, one of the things that attracted her to doing game shows was that she thought she could make a good amount of money and then spend time writing comedy without worrying about how to pay the rent. So far, her plan hasn't quite worked out. Being on a game show has been validating, though, because every time she's been on the air, she's heard from old friends and acquaintances. "I like getting acclaim from friends," she says.

In a videotape of her *Wheel* appearance, Andrea appears indigenous to the 1980s. She has long, permed hair and a classy gray wool suit. Pat Sajak introduces her to his TV audience as someone who loves to travel and learn new languages, and who works at a video dating company. She flirts with the friendly host and shows off her smarts.

In a bonus round she manages to pick a seven-letter word from only the slimmest of clues. She is given six letters, picks another four, and ends up with _ _ _ _ _ G E.

Sajak: "It's a thing. Good luck."

Andrea: "Okay, let's say luggage, baggage, cabbage."

Sajak: "Yeah, that's it, cabbage."

That one simple, overlooked, and neglected word—cabbage—landed her the keys to her very own brand-new recreational vehicle. "It was the highlight of my life," she told me. "Everything I was good at all coming together in ten seconds, right next to Pat Sajak."

As I got to know her, I realized that over the years Andrea has marinated herself in television game shows. Most of those shows demand some form of intelligence, even if it is knowledge of trivia. Scrabble is another huge part of Andrea's life, a game she plays competitively. When her ranking leveled out at around 1,300 (top-ranked players have ratings of 1,600), she grudgingly accepted that to improve she would have to study words—a hallmark of many of the best players. So she sat down and studied, memorizing every word with two letters, three letters, and on up. A lot of the top players don't bother to learn the definitions of most words—they just want to know if a word can take an *s* or an *un* or an *ed* and whether it's a *q* word that does not need a *u*—but Andrea stopped to digest each meaning. Failing to do so would be fake, phony. She delights in the romance of finding a definition in an otherwise random string of letters. "I'm just trying to make beautiful words," she says, "not trying to beat the other players."

Andrea gave up comedy in the late 1980s, when she developed an allergic reaction to secondhand cigarette smoke. Naming was her ticket out of the land of stand-up, and a pretty good way to mesh her love of words with a decent income. In the early 1990s, she moved to San Francisco, where a fledgling naming industry was growing to support what would become the Internet boom of the late 1990s. Soon Andrea came to work as a freelance namer, taking her expertise to a variety of small consulting firms like Idiom, Metaphor, Landor Associates, Interbrand, and Lexicon Branding. As we sat at that North Beach café, it struck me that naming was something I might want to try. Andrea gave me the name of one of the firms, telling me they might just hire me for a project or two.

I saw naming as a lucrative pursuit where I could use my cultural observation skills and interest in the creative side of business. My own creativity had been nurtured at the alternative elementary school I attended (where we sang the Beatles' "Back in the USSR" in rounds) but had little outlet as I got older. Naming also seemed like a natural step from journalism, which also focuses on the importance of words and of placing ideas within proper frameworks.

As a business journalist I am more attracted to the offbeat, business-culture stories than the hard-hitting, numbers-driven material that might make sense of earnings reports or analyze mergers and acquisitions. I have written articles about a novelist-turned-coach who taught CEOs how to speak clearly and effectively while raising money from investors. I first learned to surf under the tutelage of two biotechnology entrepreneurs and wrapped the episode into an article about how, for some, surfing is an integral part of the business day. Naming things seemed like a way to jump right into one of these stories, to participate instead of just observing.

Taking It to the Whiteboard

With a lead from Andrea, I got in touch with Lexicon Branding, the world's first and largest naming firm, just over the Golden Gate Bridge in Sausalito. To apply to become part of the pool of creative talent that Lexicon drew from, I sent in ten names for a new mountain bike and ten names for a new computer operating system.

The mountain bike names came naturally, as I had been riding off-road since just after the first mass-market Specialized Stumpjumper hit the trails in 1981. For bike brands I suggested Acme Designs, Rockwell Bikes, Hercules Mountain Bikes, Trajectory Cycles, Ironclad Cycles, and Armstrong Off-Road Machinery. As I made up these words I was immediately aware of how hard it was to distance a new name from existing names—and to try to differentiate a new concept radically while communicating effectively what the product was. I knew less about computer operating systems but spent a few days reading up before sending in

Iris, Helios, Mediax, Zeus, Synapse, and Axle as possibilities. I never heard what they thought of these suggestions, but in a week or two, Lexicon called me to book a day of my time.

My work at Lexicon gave me an exciting glimpse behind the corporate curtain. As I got closer to the advertising and branding industry, I came to see that well-channeled creativity fuels some of the most interesting work. Ad agencies hire the better creative talents for some sixth sense they possess, an ability to examine their own culture and appreciate it at the same time—and then to fit new ideas squarely into the context of the culture in the process of selling something. These so-called creatives play a critical role in increasingly sophisticated marketing efforts that are often far more creative than the actual products being marketed. Insofar as products sold are about buying into certain narratives and specific meanings, the industry of people who create meaning is the essential force behind the trade of consumer goods.

Lexicon's workplace was nothing terribly special, a network of offices within a three-story office building in a quiet suburban town. My own mentality changed, though, when I got there. I felt somehow privileged to play a part in what Lexicon did, excited at the notion that my ideas could have a direct impact on consumers around the world. A struggling actress who was also a first-time participant shared her own wild-eyed awe with me at lunch. "How cool is this?" she said. "This work is fun, and we're getting paid well!"

At some companies, like Lexicon, the first lesson for hired creatives is that names must be words that can be wholly owned as trademarks by the clients. Creating ownable words, they told us, was no easy feat. Lesson one held that coming up with a great name did not pose as much of a challenge as coming up with a name that could be owned and trademarked. Names like *zenith* and *Olympus* call out to be used for any product trying to be the best—but they are taken by television and camera manufacturers and are off limits. A name like *snapple* might sound like a perfect name for a new camera, but its recognition as a beverage would make owning it hard to do. To avoid falling in love with a name that someone else owns at the outset, it is critical to follow a process, a systematic method that will yield many candidates. The best naming projects begin by laying out a framework of objectives and determining what the name must convey by studying the audience it will speak to, and understanding what message the name must communicate.

Once the objectives are in place, the creative phase follows, and it can wander in many directions. The most basic creative approach focuses on brainstorming lists of adjectives and words associated with a new product or service. Some namers mine the literature associated with a new product. Naming a new chain of Tex-Mex restaurants, a namer might read cookbooks, food-industry magazines, and history texts about Route 66 and its environs. Through this process, the namer builds a database of words that have something to do with Southwestern culture (*roadhouse, mesa, burro, cowboy, turquoise, cook fire,* etc.). A namer takes in all of the documents, evaluates the culture, and sees what kind of language is bandied about, and then creates words that fit into this world. Other namers might interview customers to try to glean particularly applicable jargon.

Naming firms typically produce long lists of potential names and then determine which words they can own, which is what I did at Lexicon.

Captivated by my day trying to name a computer network at Lexicon, I wrote an article for *Wired* magazine about the naming industry. The San Francisco Bay Area proved to be something of a naming capital, and I met the majority of the players in the naming world during the course of researching the article.

The firms I met with as a journalist were as eager to meet me as I was to meet them, and once the story was done, many hired me to consult on projects. To them I came in with a journalist's skills of observation and notation. They saw me as a technologically literate member of Generation X, a key demographic for a great many products. As a freelance namer, I helped to name a chain of gas-station food marts for Chevron; computer software, hardware, and middleware; a stock-picking Web site that would eventually be sold to online broker E*Trade (it was called *ClearStation*); an online rewards program (*Netcentives*); a nutrition bar from Kraft; a phone kiosk for MCI; and a biotech startup prospecting for enzymes (*Diversa*). A good many of these projects were derailed and remained nameless.

I found myself in creative sessions of varying lengths with monologuists, performance artists, self-confessed late-night conversationalists, children's book writers, and so-called shower thinkers who all moonlighted as namers. Sometimes we had one daylong meeting and were fed lunch, other times we got an email assignment and met to present our ideas as a group. Some firms had special, artfully lit meeting rooms; at others we crowded into cramped hallways to share ideas. We worked all night sometimes, often over weekends, by email and telephone. I went to libraries where I scanned indexes in esoteric books and roamed the stacks in search of arcane texts. I spent afternoons in cafés imbibing varying levels of caffeine. Sometimes I babbled ideas into a portable tape recorder as I drove. "Here are a couple for the new mutual fund project: *Southbay Advisors, Edgeways Investments . . .*"

Each firm went at it a bit differently. At Lexicon, a company of about fifteen full-timers, the people sought to perfect methods of finding new words. Another place I consulted was called Idiom. Run by a team of two, Rick Bragdon and George Frazier, Idiom seemed more pragmatic and tended to tap freelance talent for the bulk of its work. They put less into attempting new and different methods and more into a standard process that worked again and again.

As I had found in writing the article, George and Rick, like members of the other firms, had their own proprietary means of naming. This served as a sales tool, if nothing more, to help convince clients that the $40,000 invoice was well worth paying. Rick and George were big on client engagement—bringing the client into the process of creating a new name. This was a way, I soon found out, to secure the client's sign-off on the Idiom process. Idiom worked on a lot of food-related projects that never left the drawing board (especially ones for so-called functional foods, which are imbued with nutrients and vitamins) and plenty of Internet companies that sought new names but eventually stuck with the ones they had. But Idiom's system did work, and they had a couple of impressive credits. There was the software firm they named *Wallop*—a name that came to them as they watched their clients play foosball during a break from a creative session.

During Idiom's signature "Super Session," clients spent a solid day with them, a day of in-depth participation that began with an early-morning ferry ride across San Francisco Bay. When clients arrived in the hilly hamlet of Tiburon, Rick drove them to a cozy retreat perched over the water. Inside, clients walked into a room filled with bay views and a glowing fire. This was a place, you were almost led to believe, where the blessed members of the New Economy worked like reclusive monks in harmony with themselves and with the unadulterated natural world, where they were paid well and not given to mundane worries. Rick and George covered a table with coffee, tea, freshly squeezed orange juice, and hot muffins. Most clients had flown in from some less lovely part of the country, where they toiled in corporate offices pungent with the odor of microwave popcorn. If nothing else, the location wowed and relaxed them.

Rick and George produced the semblance of a creative space, an almost Hollywood effect. Even though I was an insider, I found it easy to be lulled into the creative trance they affected. We spent the morning playing games that had names like Synonym Explosion and Blind Man's Brilliance ("name a new, all-family, fun-to-wear clothing line from Levi's made from really soft fabrics"). Every time we had more than a few minutes to concentrate on a task, they played flaky Windham Hill music on a Sony boombox.

Rick and George peppered the room with namers, wordsmiths of varying degrees, so as to make the client look as uncreative as they probably were. Yes, as a group we were more likely to churn out ideas by the dozen, but we also helped to complete an image that Idiom wanted to convey—that they had assembled a cadre of word people who, matched with particular expertise, were uniquely qualified to assist in creating a new name. There was a motherly investigative reporter for a suburban weekly tabloid, an actor and playwright who dressed in flowing, earth-toned clothes, a columnist for the *San Francisco Chronicle,* and a distinguished-looking older gentleman who had a business card that identified him as a Board Certified Omnologist. (The backside of his card defined *omnology* as "the study of everything in particular.") We performed in the mornings. We were not included in the afternoons, a period that remains mysterious.

Brainstorming sessions at Idiom were a rich mix of creativity and corporate seriousness of purpose that I came to cherish. I started to understand that you had to push to get that one winning weird idea out to the surface, out into the open and into the discussion. And that brainstorming, or blue-skying, or whiteboarding, or whatever you called it, could be approached from both scientific and artistic angles.

One day at lunch, midway through a day's work naming a snack product for a major food brand—I think it was Kraft—I met a young guy who had worked at Frito-Lay as a researcher for the snack manufacturer. He was new enough to the marketing side that he found true passion in describing the intricacies of developing chips. Television advertising spots for chips, he said, were a big part of chip-marketing campaigns, because the cadence of chip eating matched that of TV watching perfectly. Makers of chips determined an ideal size and ingredient quotient that promoted constant snacking. I learned that the taste buds and appetites of men, in particular, tended to follow a predictable pattern. According to Frito-Lay's studies, at certain hours either salt or sugar cravings are guaranteed to be present. Frito-Lay runs its ads when the savory appetites are strongest. But this Frito-Lay researcher also smirked knowingly about how plotting the whole chip research machine could be. We talked on until Rick came over and changed the subject, worried that our dialogue would undercut the Hollywood set he had so painstakingly erected.

Another product we named was a new bread product that juice seller Jamba Juice planned to market through its store chain. Before our meeting, Rick sent the three hired creatives out, assigned to capture in vibrant prose the atmosphere and activity in the stores. As I stepped back from the lunch-hour throngs pushing toward the counter, I listened carefully to the sound of whirring blenders dicing fresh fruit and smelled the sweet odor of freshly cut wheat grass. The next day, like second-graders or journalism students, we read our assignments aloud. In the meeting someone put Jamba together with the Italian word for little sandwich, *panini,* and *Jambanini* was born—which I really liked. But they went live months later with the unfortunately named *Jambola* (a name that did not last). Idiom's fundamental process centered around building consensus—something that would hold them back from producing truly revolutionary work.

I did much of the naming work I contracted at home, and gradually I began emailing my good friend Glasgow Phillips projects assigned to me by some of the San Francisco naming firms. It slowly dawned on me that there was no great secret to running a naming firm, that I could start one, too. Glasgow, a high school friend and college roommate, said he'd join me. Glasgow had written a novel called *Tuscaloosa* during his last year of college, published it at twenty-four, and gone on to study creative writing at Stanford. After a failed romance, Glasgow had fled our native California on motorcycle for Austin, Texas. He was holed up in a cheap one-bedroom apartment unsuccessfully trying to write a novel about the failed romance. He welcomed distractions.

At one point when Glasgow was in town visiting family, we attended a naming session run by an international naming and branding firm called Interbrand. We were brought into a conference room, joined by about a dozen other people, fed pizza, and paid fifty dollars for an hour's work. The group served as a communal brain that Interbrand could tap. For a mere $700 they got pages and pages of workable ideas. Most of the assembled crowd was not specifically talented in the area of verbal branding—it was a mere step up from the focus groups where people weighed in on a topic of pre-screened choice. It was the lowest rung on the naming ladder.

Working in such poor conditions, intellectually speaking, sealed the deal—we knew we could do better. We met with Glasgow's cousin Ted, a successful venture capitalist, and told him about our ideas. Ted treated us as if we were a young company in which his firm had invested $7 million. He sat us down and gave us what turned into an intense and far-reaching Business 101 lecture, sketching out what a proper pyramid-shaped business model would look like. As a venture capitalist, he was less interested in naming and branding than in how the naming process could be scaled and productized, that is, built into an efficient system that could be reliably reproduced. The exploited creatives—he called them pizza-eaters in reference to our time at Interbrand—would reside on the bottom level of the pyramid. Eventually we would sit on top.

I was being further seduced by the naming and product-launch world. I decided to put my journalism career on hold and cross over. Eventually I'd spend more than two years trading my work as a journalist (one dollar per word) to work full-time as a namer ($25,000 plus per word), living at the intersection between creativity and corporate strategy.

Before we opened for business, we needed a name for our firm. We stumbled through a couple of names for ourselves—*Alias* was one of my early favorites, and *Neology* was almost the winner— before settling on the final name. Neology is exactly what we were doing—the art of creating new words. But it didn't really sound right. I liked *Alias* because it spoke to what we did in a roundabout way, made us the less serious naming company in a world of literal, word-oriented names like Lexicon, Metaphor, and Idiom. But in the end it seemed too negative, too sinister. We called our company *Quiddity,* a word meaning character, or essence. The dictionary definition itself is lucid and concise: "that which makes a thing what it is." Quiddity came out of Glasgow's vocabulary-rich mind. I'd never heard the word before, but it seemed pleasantly antiquated and obscure, and it certainly spoke to the conjectural nature of our endeavor.

Glasgow was my partner through the thick of it—from the probative first days to the heat of the Internet chaos to the anticlimactic end. He had similarly set aside his work as a novelist to channel his energies into creating words to help our clients in the commercial sphere. We got a hands-on understanding of the role of language in business and worked mostly with Internet startup companies (as that sector of the economy was, briefly, expanding rapidly) and also for a pharmaceutical company, a hospital chain, a new investment bank, and an environmental consulting firm, among other clients. Glasgow, especially, found it continually amusing that we were paid to create words for our clients.

Having worked as a freelance creative for more than a few naming firms, I knew at least enough to explain to clients what we were doing and what we could give them in return for the money they paid us. Glasgow had never seen the inside of another naming firm, but he offered our small team the value of being an outwardly quirky character who could back up crazy antics and opinions with equal intelligence.

Glasgow's approach to client engagements differed from mine. To him, clients were new specimens to explore, new founts of knowledge from which to drink. And to share with. He never wavered in meshing his personal and professional lives, and that sometimes gave me cause for concern. One of Glasgow's strongest qualities was a self-confident streak that enabled him to posit opinions he alone held, and to defend them with integrity. He had name recognition, too—something I first noticed when we lived together in college—and people who met him just once did not forget either him or his name.

At the time we made our first sales call, I was working by day as a staff writer for a technology magazine, where I wrote articles about internal networks at large corporations, venture capital technology investing, and chief information officers, among other subjects. For the most part it was not terribly exciting material, but it gave me a good technical understanding of a lot of the client work we later did.

To expand our fledgling firm, we decided our first goal would be a simple one—to attract a client. And our first client, referred by a friend, was a provider of fiber-optic cables to tenants in large office buildings. Its name was RiserCorp, named for the hollow spaces, or risers, in buildings, through which conduit and cables run. But the client wanted us to determine whether it made sense to change the name, and if so, to what? It was our first chance to switch our operations from being hired hands to actually running the show. Heading into the meeting, I worried about how smoothly we would pull it off.

The pitch meeting with these folks took place on a speakerphone—as Glasgow sat in his bedroom in Austin, Texas, and I huddled around the phone with our two clients in San Francisco. Glasgow, ever the talkative and friendly personality, managed to be a familiar yet distant voice (like Charlie to the Angels) who could help these guys out. After the meeting, they agreed to fly him to California the next day.

I picked up Glasgow at the airport after work, and together we shot into downtown San Francisco. In the shadow of the tall building where we would meet our client, Glasgow changed into his suit. We rehearsed our roles and set off into the building. Our clients were excited to put Glasgow's face, shaved head, and pronounced nose with his name. After quick introductions, our main contact, a young and serious guy named Rodney, took us deep into the basement to show us where the fat fiber-optic cables entered the building before being channeled up to the offices through the risers.

Stepping off the elevator, we skirted a couple of immense yellow Dumpsters, walked through the dark and damp basement of this forty-story skyscraper, and stopped in front of an unmarked door. Rodney produced a key and methodically unlocked several deadbolts. As he closed the door behind us, halogen lights slowly lit the small room in front of us like dawn's faint glow, focusing our attention on rows and rows of humming servers. It looked like a vertical soundboard from a rock concert. Cooled by an ionizing filter, clear lights hanging on taut metal wires lit the room and pointed strangely skyward. My eyes moved up to the ceiling, which Rodney told us he himself had painted light blue.

Rodney paused as we took it all in. "Okay, you see how we just walked through the Dumpsters? You guys noticed all of the garbage along our way and how we are now in a sealed room filled with technology?" The little trip he had just taken us on, he explained, was an abbreviated version of the field trip he would present to future clients, tenants in the building. RiserCorp was a new-era company—a mover of bits. Its job was to plug its clients into the future, into a fiber-optic network that sent information careening along mirrored glass tubes. Rodney, a young executive on the way up, had figured out a way to impress his clientele. Based on the trip to the basement, clients would naturally think of his company as clean, organized, and futuristic. The rotting garbage outside would make his firm smell that much sweeter.

Encounters like this drew me deeper into the concept of naming and the story of a product. Rodney had not been content simply to sit and take orders for fiber-optic cabling; instead he crafted a script to add value to what his company already offered. Rodney impressed us greatly. He recognized that his company would need a good story to stand apart from its competitors, and that the story was about providing technology in a place where things were decidedly low tech. We were hired to create a few dozen names. In the end, the client kept the one it had, eventually shifting to ARC Networks. Our first client didn't embrace our output as we had hoped it would. It turned out to be far more conservative in the end, less interested in creatively altering its name in the way that Rodney's scripted subterranean adventure adjusted the typical sales pitch. But we still collected our consulting fee.

We went on to pitch work on a drug name for Glaxo Wellcome

(later known as GlaxoSmithKline) and a host of Internet startups—from one born in an incubator of new companies in San Diego that set out to streamline the way all companies bought and sold basic supplies (paper, phones, etc.) to another in Santa Cruz that created a search tool for online shopping. The engagements, done at the pace of the Internet, were often executed in mere days. Typically, we met with a group of people, usually men, in nondescript office buildings. Most often these groups were in possession of a poorly written business plan, millions of dollars, unfurnished office space, and not much else. We were often the first people they hired as consultants. Some contracts came with ridiculous price tags, like the $8,000 we were paid for spending two hours one afternoon spewing out ideas for an online jewelry site (bejewel.com, 1000ships.com, etc.).

Because there were just two of us, we rolled up our sleeves and got down to business rapidly. As we gained more work experience and signed on more clients, we realized that one of our chief duties was building consensus among client teams. Steering one, or two, or ten people in the same direction led to success. When we brainstormed on our own or with clients, we knew few boundaries—our strength lay in our ability to pull in ideas from unusual places. Yet again and again we were paid not so much to create as to serve as a neutral and objective panel, channeling our creativity into advising and ratifying our client's decision making. This was what differentiated us from mere poets and dreamers and made us, in the end, valuable to clients. In part our own newness to the field caused our creative efforts to go untapped; as time went on we got better at helping our clients to see why certain options made more sense than others.

As our company matured, we each assumed specific roles. I served as the main organizer and the straitlaced consultant who interfaced with clients. Glasgow, on the other hand, with his intellectually spastic style, proved to be the sort of secret sauce that clients came back for. He led the critical group discussions where we first quizzed our clients about their particular endeavors. His animated presence tended to put anyone who met him immediately at ease. Even in the stickiest of situations, like arriving in a corporate office park miles from home with only a vague sense of our mission, he retained his composure.

One name we created, *mPower,* for a financial planning Web site, signified a sense of *money as power,* and the notion of personal investing as a way toward personal *empowerment.* It was a short, clear name that did a good job of describing what the company was all about. We watched the name appear in the *Wall Street Journal* some months after we created it, and I rode my bike under a thirty-foot green-and-black banner that the company unfurled outside its corporate headquarters in San Francisco. It was the first time we witnessed a name we created move off the whiteboards on our office walls into the mainstream business press, and into the data streams of commerce. It was fun to witness a word travel.

For the most part the names we created—like *iWare* and *mPower*—were not injected far into the English language. They did not become part of the vernacular, the commercial patois we all use when we talk about driving our *Subarus* to the *Gap,* or opening up our *ThinkPads* to shop at *Amazon.* Coming up with the perfect name is clearly only the beginning. Unless a company devotes resources to feeding that name into the public consciousness, it will be just another word, or more often not even a word. We never had any off-the-charts blockbuster names, but we did get to see some names expand their reach.

Quiddity was an experiment we conducted. We learned on the fly, we studied, and we offered our clients what we hoped were innovative ideas. Like everyone else who was busy running around in the fever of the so-called New Economy, we had no clue that the end was near. We probably should have recognized a change in the marketplace by the time we had to start to search for work, something we had not done during our short existence. We had been a reactive organization—answering the phone when work came in, hustling to do it in record time, catching up on sleep when we could.

At Quiddity our final pitch meeting was for a transportation company that moved cargo across large bodies of water. By their calculations, one-third of the containers aboard a ship—at any given time—were empty. These are the multicolored steel boxes, often worn to a beautiful patina by the corrosive effects of salt spray on transoceanic crossings. With what can now be seen as classic Internet-era hubris, the company sought to streamline the inefficient transportation system by better coordinating the various shippers with a database-driven mechanism to be shared across the industry. Their pitch excited us; they spoke of the ease with which they would fill the world's empty containers.

It was heady stuff. Unlike the majority of our previous clients who hired Glasgow and me within hours of meeting us, this shipping concern was slow to pull the trigger—our strongest signal that the late-1990s business boom was coming to a close. In hindsight, I can see that it was a coming together of reality with nonreality. The whole Internet fever lived and breathed, rollicked along like a parade that celebrated the triumph of the *idea* over the tangible, grounded-by-gravity *thing*. But in the end there was at least some vindication for objects. Raw materials would be around for a little while longer. Actual, physical, tangible things— that had to be moved in containers and on boats and not simply beamed through the fiber-optic cables laid under the oceans— were not extinct. Perhaps there was a reason, after all, why there were empty containers—you could not so easily change supply and demand with databases, a few Excel spreadsheets, and crafty software. If nothing else, my last pitch as a namer resonated with the times.

Naming things, of course, would continue as it had before the Internet came along, just at a less fevered pace. As far as we were concerned, the rug had been pulled out from under the Internet and from under the casters of our IKEA desks. As we packed up our whiteboards, I still wanted to get back to that essential wonderment I felt when I first participated in a caffeinated brainstorm session years before.

CAMOUFLAGE AND
CODE NAMES

2

One of the first words to catch my attention was glimpsed in a short article tucked deep inside the business section of a newspaper: Porsche would soon introduce a new sport utility vehicle named *Cayenne*. Such simple facts spoke volumes. Cayenne would be the first non–sports car in the company's fifty-four-year history. That Porsche, the venerated maker of sports cars, would manufacture a sport utility vehicle seemed a radical departure for the grounded German automaker. Porsche's new car name was so fanciful, so inexplicable, and so out of character. I was intrigued.

Since 1997, Porsche had pared back its car lines and stuck to the production of just two distinct vehicles, the model 911 and the newer Boxster. A new-car launch at Porsche was certainly a change of course. A two-page article in Porsche's owner magazine, *Christophorus,* described how the head of strategy at Porsche had taken two years to create the name. The article explained that after the marketing director selected the name from some six hundred candidates, it remained a closely guarded secret for a whole year, even in-house. The marketing director had gone so far as to float the ridiculous name *Sportility* as a red herring to throw off inquisitive car trade magazines.

According to the story Porsche laid out, *Cayenne* rapidly became the winning name internally—a name that would be understood worldwide as a synonym for spiciness and adventure that would describe the characteristics of the new off-road SUV. Like Porsche's Carrera, the Spanish word for "race," Cayenne's marketing leader claimed to have chosen a term that would be immediately understood in almost every language and was associated with particularly spirited qualities. The name reportedly galvanized Porsche forces inside the company and brought an esprit de corps to the car launch efforts.

Porsche CEO Wendelin Wiedeking backed the name choice. To him, *Cayenne* was a name on par with the company's other suite of names—like *Carrera, Targa,* and *Boxster*—some of which are model names and others body styles. Those names, he said, all dovetailed inseparably with the Porsche brand name and made a decisive contribution to the strong image and success of these products. But it was less clear how *Cayenne* fit in. The name for the new SUV had to reflect the Porsche product philosophy both on- and off-road: "We are convinced that the combination of Porsche and Cayenne as a model designation radiates true strength, dynamism, fascination, and emotions and will continue the great tradition of legendary names," he said.

A strict etymology of the word showed that *cayenne* was borrowed from a Native American language, originally spelled *kyinha* and then *cayan*. The cayenne chili is long and thin with a sharp point and ranges in size from half an inch to seven inches in length. Cayenne peppers are believed to have returned with members of Columbus's second voyage to the Americas and then spread throughout Europe as a spice.

To me, the name did not seem like an auspicious start. It didn't refer to a body style, to a famous race, or to a part of the car, and it was not a number as were most Porsche automobiles. It veered off into the abstract. The name would never stand on its own but as the two-named corporate binomial *Porsche Cayenne*. Cayenne was no great linguistic leap forward for Porsche.

The automobile marketplace has slowly been reconfigured into a pack of half-truths. Volvo, the venerated Swedish automaker, and British carmakers Jaguar and Land Rover are now but divisions of Ford Motor Company. Audi is no longer a stand-alone company but a luxury sister brand to Volkswagen. Each of these European brands has historically possessed unique qualities; now most of them are designed in the United States and built in Mexico. While rivals such as Saab (a division of GM) and Aston Martin (owned by Ford) have been gobbled up by global players, Porsche continues to thrive as a small, niche performance car producer. Ford bought Volvo for its brand image; in one word: safety. Porsche could easily end up as a one-word signifier like Volvo, under the umbrella of some other major car company. What preoccupied me as I started to investigate the Cayenne story was this question: Was this new car the first step in that unfortunate process—when the name would live on, but the essence would slowly die off?

As a journalist, the accepted way to approach a company you plan to write about is to contact its press relations department. My first contact at Porsche headquarters in Stuttgart, Germany, gave his name simply as "Schwartz." We played international telephone tag until he reached me on a crackling line to my cell phone early one morning. I explained my interest in learning more about the Cayenne launch and specifically the name. Schwartz listened attentively and respectfully. "I am sorry, that will not be possible, Mr. Frankel," he stated dryly in heavily accented English.

I called on Schwartz's superiors, hoping to move my query up the chain of command. Not having heard back from the public relations department, I sent a letter directly to several Porsche executives. I received a fax from the head of public relations, Michael Schimpke, who thanked me for considering the story of Porsche but declined to work with me on it. He wrote, "We prefer to bring the Sports Utility Vehicle named Cayenne into the market before speaking about strategy details surrounding this car in depths [sic]."

I told him I was simply interested in finding out how and why Porsche had come to call its new car Cayenne. I did not want or need to see the car at all. Again, Mr. Schimpke declined to assist me in my investigation.

At that point I figured that the only way to gain an audience with Porsche would be to present my case in person. I wanted to get a better understanding of the Porsche strategy, and maybe, just a little bit, "to live the brand," not only to track a name but to track the product, too. I would be in Europe to interview some marketers in London and meet up with some friends in Italy anyway, so I called Porsche once again to try to set up a meeting with Mr. Schimpke. I faxed my plans and received a reply stating that he would be in Italy at the launch of the Carrera 4S. As I was myself in Italy at the time, and it is a relatively small country, I called Mr. Schimpke's assistant to ask where the launch would be.

"In the north or the south?" I asked

"In the middle," she told me.

"Oh, great," I said. "I am in Florence, in the middle."

She warned that he would be in meetings all day during this car launch. We kept talking, and she finally advised me to call the following day and said that maybe she could patch me through to her boss. I suspected immediately that the Italy car launch was a ruse to throw me off the trail. I packed my bags and hopped on an overnight train from Florence to Munich and then on to Stuttgart, hoping to meet Schimpke at Porsche headquarters.

Unknowingly, I had bought not a seat on the train but a bunk bed—or couchette—and was forced to lie down in a compartment crammed with three others and try to sleep as the train thundered out of Florence and into the dark night. The conductor told me to watch out for thieves, so I tied a shoelace to my duffel bag before crashing for the night. A guy sleeping across from me was dressed in pressed slacks and a leather jacket two sizes too large. As we pitched into the Munich train station, he removed a black bottle of Drakkar Noir cologne, which he had duct-taped shut. He sprayed his chest under the leather jacket, and then covered his hands and pushed them through his hair and wiped his face. My fellow "business traveler" was ready for his next sales call.

On the commuter train to Stuttgart, a well-dressed young guy and girl walked up to my seat and offered me a pad of white Post-it notes. The notes were imprinted with the brand name *Vodafone,* below which was a tag line that read "How are you?" in English. A million Post-it notes would spread . . . How are *you*? How *are* you? *How* are you?

I knew it wasn't likely that Porsche would be so interested in gaining publicity for the forthcoming car that they would hand me a set of keys so I could drive a prototype down the Autobahn and weigh in on the car's handling abilities. But I would soon find out that Porsche's real concern was that I was a spy for the automotive press, on my own stealth mission to steal heavily guarded trade secrets.

After checking into my hotel in Stuttgart, I took a shower and put on the suit that I had carried all the way from home for the explicit purpose of wearing it to an unscheduled interview at Porsche. I took the light-rail S-Bahn train to a station called Neuwirtshaus, more familiarly known as Porsche Platz. The entire area said *Porsche*. There is a large dealership next door to the corporate headquarters, a small museum, and a factory where

911 and Boxster models are made. A brochure explained that "here, the history and stories involving Porsche brand are close enough to touch." I went into the gallery-size museum and looked at the many cars organized in chronological order. It was somewhat sterile and unimpressive, a mere show of artifacts with no peek into the fabrication process. I walked around the museum and summoned the conviction to proceed with my plan to somehow get invited into the looming Porsche office building.

A jovial, Turkish-born guard who wore a blue sweatshirt with a Porsche logo on it and proclaimed his friendship with the U.S.A. greeted me in the guardhouse. He controlled a switch that brought a red-and-white gate up and down. I asked the guard to call Mr. Schimpke and announce my arrival, which he dutifully did.

"You have surprised me, Mr. Frankel," Schimpke said by way of introduction. Mr. Schimpke told me he was somewhere on the outskirts of the city, available only on his cell phone and unable to meet with me. But I conducted an interview nonetheless, standing in the guardhouse. We spoke for about half an hour as I hovered above my new friend the guard, cradled the phone against my left shoulder, scribbled notes on a note pad, and kept an eye out for an errant Cayenne.

Schimpke started by telling me that Porsche was itself publishing a book (that would be released with the car) about the marketing and engineering of the Cayenne. I asked him why, in the case of Porsche's last car launch, the Boxster, the company so easily cooperated with the press. The Boxster was unveiled in 1993 and was available in 1996. Schimpke said that at the time the company was in need of good press, because it had been suffering economically. "We had a great interest in letting people know that this car was the future," he told me.

I asked him where the car name came from, and he said that, as a matter of fact, Porsche had made a deal with its advertising agency not to speak at all about the naming process. It would be a sealed issue.

I had read statements from Porsche Cars of North America, the only licensed importer into the United States, that the real reason Porsche had pursued an SUV was to produce sales and ensure that the company would remain independent and able to continue making its classic line of cars. CEO Wiedeking wanted to double the size of the company, and he saw Americans' insatiable demand for SUVs as the key to realizing that goal.

When I asked Schimpke whether it was unseemly for Porsche to pander to demand, he responded by evading the question and offering me just a glimpse of Porsche's PR strategy. "We want to avoid controversy . . . the questions of 'Should a sports car manufacturer build an SUV?' and 'Let's see if it drives as good as it looks.' What we like is to bring the car into the market and discuss it then. We prefer conversations started by ourselves. . . . It's not about secrecy. We like to be able to bring it into the market and then give the full reality of it. Otherwise we have to say 'Believe me.' There is a belief that whatever Porsche does, it does well. And it will be again so."

I pushed him to reveal some information about the new car launch, or at least to tell me why he was being so tight-lipped about it. When you are talking to a public relations professional like Mr. Schimpke, you have to suspect that every word he utters is a form of spin, but I sort of believed him when he spoke about his reasons for waiting to discuss more.

As I was talking to Schimpke on the phone in the guardhouse, a half-dozen brand-new 911s roared past the entry gate, driven by men in white shirts, each car giving off the characteristic purr from its brand-new engine. Growing up, I was never a car fanatic, like some of my friends, but I did over time gain a sense of awe for the classic, iconic Porsche 911 with its timeless, wavelike frame. It's a car with a distinctive sound, an electronic humming purr I can recognize a block away. In high school, one friend's father owned a sleek black 911 SC. On the rare weekend when his parents left town, we secretly rolled the car out for late-night, fast-paced and reckless forays into the hills above his house. We began our midnight missions by using masking tape to identify the angle of each parked wheel. We wrote out a list of all movable objects in the car so that once we were home we could replace each item in the car and conceal our stealthy usage. As I held on with the seatbelt tight against my chest, my friend accelerated through the dark, tight turns. He was as thrilled by the act of driving as by the extreme consequences that any driving error would bring. Over the years, the 911 presented itself to me as a perfectly built machine—spartan in design and well crafted throughout. A Porsche, in short.

At 1:00 p.m. I witnessed the changing of the crews. Dozens of German men walked by the door on the way out, followed by a similar influx of workers, all flashing identification cards. Standing in the guardhouse asking Schimpke to reveal some part of the Porsche naming strategy—to reveal anything, really, about how Porsche came up with the name—I slowly realized that I was living the strategy. The strategy was to be silent to the press, to not enter the conversation, as Schimpke put it. And to be super-stealthy—this was the essence of the launch. By being coy with me, he was leading my interest further along.

Because I could barely get Schimpke to talk to me, let alone invite me in for a cup of coffee, I left the guardhouse and wandered around the periphery of the Porsche campus, which has a number of gray metallic-ribbed buildings. Employees wearing silver Porsche jumpsuits walked by carrying Siemens phones clipped to their coveralls. When I asked about the Cayenne, I was met with hunched shoulders and indifferent looks. I dropped by the Porsche dealership nearby, where a 911 had been cut in half lengthwise, showing a cross-section of this $70,000 car. I approached a sales-woman, who would not so much as acknowledge the launch of the Cayenne. It was a code word that was met with silence.

Car naming has been one of the richest areas of product naming. Cars are the highest-cost brand-name products that most people buy in a lifetime. People tend to associate cars, more than most material objects, with particular lifestyles: cruising goes with Chevy muscle cars, soccer moms with minivans, ten-gallon hats with two-ton pickups, yuppies with BMWs. Car names have included hard-to-pronounce names (*Hyundai*), names misspelled to promote trademark ownership (*Chevrolet Prizm, Pontiac Aztek*), and poorly translated names (in Mexico the Chevrolet Nova was read as "no va," as in "doesn't go").

The history of naming cars, it turns out, is filled with secrecy, but I found at least one revelatory exchange. In October 1955, an employee named Robert B. Young in the market research department at Ford Motor Company wrote a letter to the poet Marianne Moore in which he explained that Ford wanted to hire her to create new names for an impending car launch. In what turned into an almost yearlong correspondence, Moore, an award-winning modernist poet known for inventing words and poetical forms, traded witty exchanges with Young. Moore and Young's letters are the most literary epistolary exchange in naming history. They show a naming process that has not really changed in the past fifty years, although the names have.

In his first note, Young wrote, "This morning we find ourselves with a problem which, strangely enough, is more in the field of words and the fragile meaning of words than in car-making." He continued: "Our dilemma is a name for a rather important new series of cars. We should like this name to be more than a label. Specifically, we should like it to have a compelling quality in itself and by itself. To convey, through association or other conjuration, some visceral feeling of elegance, fleetness, and advanced features and design. A name, in short, that flashed a dramatically desirable picture in people's minds." He ended his first note to Moore: "In summary, all we want is a colossal name (another 'Thunderbird' would be fine)."

Moore, over the course of several months, sent in a few suggestions. Her first was the Ford *Silver Sword,* named after a flower. Young replied, "Shipment 1 was fine and we would like to luxuriate in more of same." He continued, "We have sought your help to get an approach quite different from our own. In short we should like suggestions that we ourselves would not have arrived at."

Young sent Moore some drawings and she sent more ideas: the *Impeccable,* the *Resilient Bullet,* the Ford *Fabergé.* She added in one letter, "Please do not feel that memoranda from me need acknowledgment. I am not working day and night for you; I feel that etymological hits are partially accidental." Moore sent others: *Mongoose, Civique, Anticipator, Dearborn Diamanté.* Her last missive had just one suggestion: *Utopian Turtletop.* In response to this final suggestion, Ford sent her a floral tribute of two dozen roses and a note that read, "To our favorite Turtletopper."

In Young's last letter to Moore, he noted that the "art of precise word picking is rarely joined with the mechanical genius of our automotive personnel. Your aid in this respect has been invaluable." He signed the letter, "Your faithful utopian." Nearly a year passed, and then Ford announced its new car, selected from more than six thousand names (including Moore's): It was the Ford *Edsel,* named after Henry Ford's only son. The Edsel was heavily promoted by Ford with a campaign that stated, "Once you've seen it, you'll never forget it. Once you've owned it, you'll never want to change." Ford launched the ill-fated car during a recession, and its large size and technical problems caused sales to founder.

Ford pulled the car out of production three years later, but the name lived on as a symbol of failure.

Even as Young sent Moore some sketches, he noted that there was an air of secrecy at Ford: "Advance designs in Dearborn are something approaching the Sacred. But perhaps the enclosed sketches will serve the purpose. They are not IT, but they convey the feeling." Such paranoia, I had seen, is as hard-wired into the auto industry as the search for the next big car.

Months after my journey to Stuttgart, after the car's public unveiling, I would get a chance to drive a brand new Cayenne—one painted Lapis Blue Metallic with a Sand Beige interior. It closely resembled Nissan's new Murano SUV (named for the sculpted glass made near Venice, Italy), which was selling for half the price. I would leave the showroom, not so sure that Cayenne was a "colossal name" nor a Thunderbird that flashed a "dramatically desirable picture in people's minds."

With Porsche I made the mistake of approaching the company directly—and in not finding the word's actual creators. No company likes to admit that it has turned to outsiders for creative advice, but it was the outsiders I needed to speak with. Lexicon, naturally, was the first place to stop—to see what was going on, and find out what words they were creating and sending out into the world.

BLACKBERRY: SENDING A QUICK MESSAGE

3

One day some months after we closed up shop at Quiddity, I dropped by Lexicon to watch a group conduct its final creative meeting for a pro bono project. Founder David Placek was in his element, running the meeting with several Lexicon staffers and his veteran creative lieutenant, Steve Price. Lexicon's staff was in the process of naming a new women's institute that would "nurture, encourage, and support young women in careers in science, math, and engineering." The main objective for the name was to establish credibility and help the institute raise funds amid the moneyed and tech-heavy culture of Silicon Valley.

Placek started the meeting by asking, simply, "Where is the PowerBook, the Laser Tag, the black hole?" In posing such a question, he invoked Lexicon shorthand. He wanted to know which name had the potential to be an archetypal name that invents a category—like PowerBook, which Lexicon created for Apple. He wanted to know which name was simply the best way to say something—like Laser Tag, a game that started out awkwardly as *Photon*. Similarly, black holes were at first called "totally gravitational collapsed objects" and defined as collapsed stars with incredibly strong gravitational pull. No one could wrap his head around this term until someone rechristened the phenomena *black holes*—objects from which light could not escape. Popular astrophysics has never been the same. The black hole, in short, provides a handy lesson in the power of a good name.

This meeting concluded Lexicon's broad-based discovery and research program, and one of Lexicon's staffers had taped fifty names to the wall in the vault, the room where these sorts of creative meetings take place. One by one, the group went through the names and discussed which ones might work, and which ones would not cut it.

Jaya, a word that means "victory" in Sanskrit, was the name that fell farthest off-center on the spectrum presented. *Precisive, StarField,* and *LeftBrain* also got air time. Steve Price made a suggestion: "We should not call out how smart these people are—it seems redundant, childish." Underlying the discussion was the real role of this organization, and the larger role of women in the sciences.

Lift got kicked around, then dismissed because it sounded like a name for a bra. What about *BrightCircle?* "Sounds too much like a Disney film," said Placek. *Kendra,* the Greek word for "knowing woman," got some interest, too. By the end of the meeting the room began to smell strongly of a blueberry scent emitted from the marking pens used to take notes. The group effectively whittled the list to around thirty-two candidates, but the project was far from complete. The client came in the next week to review the names, but none stuck. Apparently there would be no PowerBook, no black hole, and no Laser Tag coming from Lexicon on that particular project. The client didn't take any of Lexicon's choices; the organization is now known as WiSTEM (for Women in Science, Technology, Engineering, and Mathematics).

In the small but lucrative offshoot of the advertising and branding industry in which names are created for products and services, Lexicon's clients pay for mainly one commodity: new brand names produced through divergent, nonlinear thinking. The largest naming firm in the world, Lexicon claims to have pioneered an evolving system to produce divergent thinking that works. Placek hatched Lexicon in 1984 as a service that he ran frugally out of his San Francisco apartment. Over the next several years he ramped up his operations, and these days the firm works out of several offices in the foggy enclave of Sausalito, a small town just north of San Francisco.

For someone whose business is creativity, Placek's daily dress is conservative by California standards—blue jeans, leather slip-on shoes, and white, pressed Oxford cloth shirts. A former freelance namer likens Placek's look to that of a Catholic schoolboy. Placek typically shows up at seven each morning and puts in seventy-hour weeks while aiming each day to set aside three or four hours to do creative work—which might involve coaching others about how to approach new naming projects creatively, or sitting down and working on creating names himself, which he finds relaxing.

At Lexicon, seventeen staff members work in what is an essentially nonhierarchical firm, but the core Lexicon creative team is just four guys—David Placek, Steve Price, Marc Hershon, and Bob Cohen—who have worked together for more than ten years. For any project it faces, this main team tends to do the heavy lifting.

Lexicon's staff includes a couple of linguistics Ph.D.s, each of whom lives in a half-commercial, half-academic world, and several researchers, with one devoted entirely to legal research. There isn't a lot of turnover. Hershon hooked up with Placek while he was trying to succeed as a screenwriter and worked as a freelance creative for Placek back in 1988, and he brought in Steve Price, who was working as a local stage actor. Today both manage to pursue their artistic interests on the side.

The organizational chart at Lexicon may be flat, but it is clear that Placek rules the roost. Placek did some time in advertising proper before deciding, and committing to the idea—a bit of a gamble at the time—that the world needed a firm whose sole mandate was to come up with names. He started in advertising and worked for five years at Foote, Cone & Belding—a onetime agency powerhouse with anchor clients like Levi's. At Foote, Cone it was the small workgroups that captured Placek's attention. Among other things, he noticed that small groups executed much of the best work, and that not every small group worked as efficiently as the next.

After five years at Foote, Cone, Placek headed to another firm, S&O Consultants, which asked him to establish a new-products group. There he cut his teeth creating names for new products. Through his work at this firm he saw that there was a need for a service devoted exclusively to creating new names. And, over time, his firm did just that. "I want to be known for 'If you want a great name that will increase the likelihood that you will have a great brand—go to Lexicon,' " says Placek.

Since 1984, Lexicon has created more than 1,500 names for products and services—many of them now household names. When Apple Computer hired Lexicon in the late 1980s, it had just launched a heavy, slow, portable machine, the Macintosh Portable. It weighed seventeen pounds and was quickly dubbed "the luggable." For its next machine, a lighter and faster model, Apple wanted a new name.

Lexicon began working with the known terms *laptop* and *notebook* and brought together focus groups of users of competitive products. In 1991, the PowerBook was born, linking the word *book,* a small product that holds a lot of information, with *power,* a word that emerged from focus groups. "What you have in *Power-Book,*" says Placek, "is two things that are very common but are not used together." The PowerBook captured attention. When people talked about PowerBook, the word radiated. People no longer simply used computers, or even laptops—but PowerBooks. A new noun was born. Lexicon went on to create other names for Apple, none of which took off in quite the same way, such as *Centrus, Quadra,* and *QuickTake,* underlining the fact that great names succeed best when backed up by great, niche-defining products.

In 1993, Lexicon created the name Pentium, evoking a fifth-generation (from the Greek *pente*) chip with resonance as an element (like vanadium). Andrew Chaikin, a freelance namer who had nothing to do with the naming of Intel's chip, told me it ranks as one of his favorite names: "Pentium . . . Pentium! That is a great word," he said. "It triggers some brain synapse. Sure, they could have named it the '586' chip—but let me just list a few things I think about when I hear *Pentium.* It sounds like it's out of a James Bond movie. It feels hard and elemental. It sounds like some rare element, something that can be found on the periodic table of the elements alongside titanium and selenium. It's like some substance that has to be mined in Africa and sells for $500 an ounce. It gleams." He waited a few seconds: "All these meanings evoked by three syllables! Names crystallize—they express. As a namer you try to compress the inner nature of something into a small package." And Pentium impressed more than those in the industry. Intel—once a staid chipmaker whose products were numbered, not named—leveraged Pentium Processors into a brand and joined it with the massive "Intel Inside" so-called ingredient marketing campaign.

Lexicon has a number of huge successes to its credit among

the 1,500 names it has created; Embassy Suites hotels, Levi's Slates Dress Slacks, Vibrance Shampoo, Subaru's Forester and Outback all-wheel-drive vehicles, and Zima, a clear malt beverage. When Coca-Cola wanted a name for a new purified bottled water, it turned to Lexicon. Lexicon's feeling was that if Coca-Cola were to succeed, it would need to gain distance from the water already out there, whose labels all said to Placek "glacier-fed, green water, deep, ice, cool." Faced with the postmodern task of naming water, Lexicon came up with *Dasani*. To Paul Taylor, Coca-Cola's director of hydration (an undoubtedly serious post), the word suggests freshness, motion, fluidity, vitality, and essence of life. It's so well separated from Coke that you have to look closely to notice that Dasani is a Coke sub-brand.

Lexicon has launched more than its share of new words into the global marketplace. Typical engagements yield several thousand possible names, some of which are reused in later assignments. A company that pays for the creation of a new name may browse the entire list of names generated during its project, but it purchases only the names it plans to use. Prices start at $45,000 per name, a figure that sounds high. Yet when the right name is created effectively and exhaustively, a lot goes into it. And the challenge for Lexicon is that though it may be a word factory, every word it produces is different from the last. You don't generate good creative material by staying in the same place.

Paging Lexicon

In 1998, when Dave Werezak flew from Waterloo, Ontario, to meet with Lexicon in its Sausalito offices, he brought with him a functioning prototype of a new device invented by his company. It was a startling little square box—not much bigger than a standard pager—that would let people receive and send email wirelessly from pretty much anywhere. The device was about two inches high by four inches wide, yet a radio transceiver was packed inside, and its surface was big enough to hold a small keyboard and a miniature screen. Werezak's company, Research In Motion (RIM), had just struck an initial deal with Southwestern Bell to market the new device to customers in the United States. Around his company was a pervasive feeling that the little tool might take off.

Unlike the flash-in-the-pan Internet launches in the late 1990s, RIM plodded along slowly and successfully for more than a decade before bringing its wireless email product to market. Research—as in the name Research In Motion—is a key part of the company. The idea for the wireless system dates back to 1989, when RIM first worked on an outsourced project for Hewlett-Packard, writing software to let users run wireless email accounts. The bulk of RIM's sales always had come from contract engineering, like manufacturing wireless modems for third parties. But as RIM focused more on wireless data, it turned to creating and manufacturing its own devices. The first RIM internal product was a two-way pager—the RIM 900.

Other pager companies had tried—and failed—to combine email with pagers, and by the early 1990s many in the industry saw wireless email as a product that people did not really want or need. RIM took a different tack. Its new product—the prototype Dave Werezak was about to show Lexicon—was not just a pager but an email management system that routed email and coordinated wired and unwired email. It let users send and receive email from almost anywhere, in real time, continuously. For the first time the new device would tap people into their corporate networks, too, so that a copy of every email sent to their office computer would be forwarded to them, wherever they might be. The key to the success of RIM's device was an entire integrated system that included the software that sat on a main server or PC and service from a wireless carrier to synchronize wireless email and regular email. As email became pivotal to many workers' daily workload and many found themselves out of the office and on the road, being constantly connected was a major attraction. *Customers would want this.*

As RIM's marketing vice president, Werezak oversaw the naming process and recognized that the rapidly expanding mobile telecommunications industry was filled with brand names that, while very descriptive, all sounded alike. Typical of the market was Motorola's 1996 rollout, the PageWriter 2000. Now in the Smithsonian, its most vital component was not its name. For RIM, a recognizable brand name would be a major asset.

When challenging an incumbent in the marketplace, a new product must work harder just to be heard. While established players often have the resources and positioning to select the best operating plan, new competitors must turn to specialized treatment. A wealthy baseball team like the New York Yankees can buy any player it wants; a less well-off team like the Oakland Athletics has to find and groom new players. Social psychologists refer to this difference in approach as "treatment effects and selection effects," and it is a helpful way to think of naming and how it influences the success of product launches. RIM's product would go up against Motorola's next effort, and its naming project—its treatment—would be critical to gaining success. A Motorola product would be guided by selection, and Motorola could sit on its laurels and call its new product the *Communicator*. For RIM this type of name would never gain exposure—it would be just another dull-named product from an obscure Canadian company.

Around RIM, employees working in stealth mode called their forthcoming system *PocketLink*. Although external focus groups were gravitating toward the name, Werezak and his team thought such a name would be the wrong way to go—it would do nothing to differentiate the new product or the company. "Part of the reason we didn't use *PocketLink* was that it was a descriptive name, and the category (at the time) was mostly populated with descriptive names. To stand apart, we wanted instead to pursue a connotative name for the brand," Werezak says. "As first mover in the market, we had an opportunity to build a brand around a new category." Werezak says RIM knew it wanted the naming done right, so it called Lexicon.

After Werezak and his team at RIM signed on as Lexicon clients, Placek and his colleague Marc Hershon began their inquiry process. The first stage of discovery at Lexicon involves understanding the product. "We, as a company, want to learn everything there is to know about a particular product or service or component before we start naming," says Placek. "So we like to get briefed by engineers and understand the technology behind it. Sometimes there is a word or metaphor in the technology that we use, or flip that directly into a consumer brand." The chip that became Pentium was code-named 586, for example, giving Pentium its *pente* prefix.

Werezak met with Placek and Hershon to describe fully just how PocketLink worked. Powered by the Intel 386 chip, which once powered entire desktop computers, the major underlying technological breakthrough of the diminutive device was its ability to forward email sent through a desktop email system to a wireless network that fed off simple 900-megahertz radio waves. It was a superb, innovative technology and a superb, innovative idea. The name had to speak to both.

Placek and Hershon checked out PocketLink and sent a few messages from Werezak's prototype back to some people at RIM headquarters in Canada. It worked. Lexicon fired up its creative engines, which were largely built around the success of small-group thinking that Placek had studied since his earliest days in the field.

Creativity Comes in Small Packages

At his first advertising agency job, Placek sought to understand how teams solve problems, and he wanted to discover or uncover methods to generate productive group creativity. The agency gave Placek latitude and time to study small groups, and he found helpful insights from places like NASA and a leading California-based think tank, the RAND Corporation. With his focus and interest in small groups, other account groups at the agency sent projects to Placek, including accounts like Dial Soap, Pacific Telephone and Telegraph, Levi's, and the Clorox Company. The new-products group involved him in a lot of projects that included creating new product names—an area he found especially fertile for experimenting with small-group dynamics.

From his experience in seeing how creativity was harnessed in the context of small teams, Placek developed the somewhat intangible commodity known as divergent thinking. The concept itself goes by a range of names—*out-of-the-box, untethered, blue-sky thinking*. When it's really put into practice, though, and not merely a buzzword, divergent thinking means finding new ways to think about things. Lexicon's mandate is to bring customers into this new way of thinking. In an ideal scenario, Lexicon's client has a product that deviates from the mass of products already out there, and Lexicon can apply ideas that similarly vary from those already in play to this product.

"In smaller companies like Lexicon," Placek told me, "you do not have a load of bureaucracy that out of necessity dulls people's creativity and a team's creativity. The creativity index goes up at a small firm. The challenge is, how do you stimulate the creativity of your people? My interest is in making teams work, and this has led us to be successful. I think the culture at Lexicon is one of creativity."

Placek's interest in the creativity of small groups and an awareness of the need for product naming, not an overarching love of words, led him to start Lexicon. To many people, the idea of creating names for a living sounds like a dream job. And indeed Lexicon gets many letters each month that go something like: *I've always been into words—WORDS, yeah!, I collect interesting names and palindromes, I've written a book on dog names through history, I'm an amateur poet, I LOVE how words express emotions* . . . But Placek has no interest in hiring word nerds—he says he looks for people who can solve complex problems. "A love of words for someone who names might be like a love of paint for a painter—the love of the raw resource does not necessarily indicate any ability to create with that resource," says Placek's colleague Marc Hershon.

"The kinds of people who succeed at this are people who want to address opportunities and solve problems. Sure, we can use prefixes to solve problems, but there is not a lot of oohing and aahing that goes on here at Lexicon. This is about building new brands and creating new markets," says Placek. "Good namers," in Placek's view, "have very well-rounded perspectives."

Until recently, Lexicon made frequent use of external talent, drawing on various creative people like poets, actors, musicians, and performance artists—basically anyone who had a brain that could be tapped for good words (including Andrea Michaels and me). People were paid a daily fee to come in and participate in group sessions. The names they generated stayed with Lexicon and filled their expanding database. If a name didn't make it for a certain project, it could be tagged and filed electronically for future reference. The intent, says Steve Price, was to bring in a diversity of viewpoints to solve a problem. But over time, Price—who led a lot of the daylong group sessions—says he sensed diminishing returns. Price's role, as someone who often ran meetings in Lexicon's creative room, was to constantly steer people away from consensus.

Consensus poses an interesting dilemma. It's the point around which much creative work pivots. As William Whyte wrote in his classic *The Organization Man*, "It is the price of progress that there never can be complete consensus. All creative advances are essentially a departure from agreed-upon ways of looking at things, and to overemphasize the agreed-upon is to further legitimize the hostility to that creativity upon which we all ultimately depend."

From the first days when he studied small-group dynamics, Placek realized that if you put a group together in a room, after a while they start to think and act alike. "What we are fighting here, what you always fight within the creative process, is a move toward commonality and away from diversity and divergent thinking." Small groups still produce most of the solutions at Lexicon, but Placek has found that they need to be separated continually. Bringing in people who hailed from a range of disciplines seemed to work for a number of years, but eventually it became clear that, despite an initial variance of viewpoints, within an hour or two even the most creative people tended toward groupthink.

The term *groupthink* is generally attributed to Yale psychologist Irving L. Janis, a pioneer in the study of social dynamics. In 1972, he called groupthink "a mode of thinking that people engage in when they are deeply involved in a cohesive in-group, when members' strivings for unanimity override their motivation to realistically appraise alternative courses of action." Janis said groupthink could be found whenever institutions made difficult decisions, and he cited NASA and the U.S. Armed Forces as two examples of groups often stymied by groupthink. It's ironic, because any name would have to encourage a sort of consumer-at-large group-think—but getting to the final decision would have to be devoid of groupthink. It's almost a given that companies involved in naming projects fall prey to groupthink. But Lexicon's mission is to avoid it.

Masking assignments and carefully planned research are two ways to avoid the pitfalls of groupthink. During my first day in a creative session at Lexicon, I was impressed by the level of prepa-ration that worked to ensure that our ideas remained fresh. We constantly approached the problem from new and different an-gles. Price led the group, joined by his colleague Hershon and four of us brought in from the outside world. After I learned a lit-tle bit about Lexicon's processes, it dawned on me that the entire day could have served a different purpose from the one we thought we were engaged in. We were told that we were naming a computer network, but once I better understood Lexicon's techniques, I realized that we could have been naming a cellular phone, or a new consulting firm, or a two-way pager. Flush with Internet money, Placek could simply have designated our day as one to test certain ideas about how small groups work.

Maintaining a diversity of viewpoints is still an underlying phi-losophy governing creativity at Lexicon. The approach, though, is no longer dependent on the ideas of outsiders but on the in-house team that works on a project in its discovery phase. Break-ing out of static thought is key to creativity.

"The creative process is by definition sloppy," says Hershon. Promoting divergent thinking often means breaking into separate teams to work on the same project, or even misleading staff mem-bers into believing they are preparing a name for one client when it may be meant for another. Lexicon's staff is as susceptible to marketing as are true consumers. Knowing they are working on a project for Hewlett-Packard, they will likely think in a different way than on a project for Apple, just as a Nike project will shape choices in a way an Adidas project would not. "You can learn so much by transferring principles from one thing to another," says Placek.

So when Werezak of Research In Motion came calling, Placek and Hershon met with him discreetly—keeping the rest of the firm in the dark about their new client. It's a tried-and-true method for Placek, who likes to, as he says, shift the creative target. For Research In Motion, he sent off some staff to name a scholastic version of a handheld computer. Others were told to create a name for what he called "a brand-new way of communicating." Another group worked on naming a medical diagnostic tool.

"We can always come back to the straightforward approach," says Placek. "That is the relatively easy ground to cover. But we're really paid to step back and say, 'How can we get to higher ground here?'" By exploring masked assignments, the Lexicon team examines what Hershon calls "fractal versions" of the larger project. Mathematician Benoit Mandelbrot coined the term *fractal* (from the Latin word *fractus*) in 1975, after identifying the idea that nature exhibits irregular shapes—unlike squares and triangles, more like broken stones—that have the same degree of non-regularity on all scales. A straightforward or geometric takeoff on PocketLink would be to look at products that do similar things: other pagers, for example. A fractal version would spin off a bit further afield, while maintaining a connection—albeit an irregular one—to the original project.

Fractal products, or masked assignments, have to be closely related so that their solutions will have parallel meanings and possess intrinsic value. Although the word *Pentium* held a reference to Intel's fifth-generation microprocessor, it also maintained word parts that would make it seem fast and powerful. It could have been a pair of skis or a powerful car and still have passed an intrinsic-value "sniff test," as Hershon calls it. By the same reasoning, the masked assignments share some intrinsic quality with the product being named.

"Our clients pay us to think beyond where they thought," Placek told me. And to do this, Lexicon has to go a long way into its discovery process. For PocketLink, Lexicon began by asking, What's the marketplace going to look like in two, five, or ten years? Will everyone have a PocketLink in his or her pocket? Will everyone have a cell phone? How will the marketplace mutate? This is the science fiction side of naming, where the namer is called on to predict future trends—or at least attempt to do so.

Would PocketLink remain a luxury item, or would it become a necessity? Would it quickly saturate the marketplace like the television, which spread from a 9 percent saturation of U.S. households in 1950 to 90 percent saturation in 1962? Or would it creep out like the telephone, which, although introduced in 1877, had by 1921 penetrated just 30 percent of households. Saturation is a point at which few markets are still open, and demand turns downward. Where would PocketLink fall on the Engel curve, a model that separates luxuries from necessities?

Lexicon asks these questions to help it understand the client's product, and also to qualify each client before signing on. "I am always looking to answer—'Is this product going to move the marketplace? Is this client team committed to building a brand?'" says Placek. Over the two-month project, Lexicon found Werezak to be a "conceptual" client, one able to get behind the Lexicon process and visualize how a word would evolve to become a brand.

As with most professional services firms, Lexicon has found that some clients retain the company as a partner—a trusted adviser to bring into discussions—and others treat it as simply an outside vendor. Companies that recognize the vital importance of creating a solid brand name tend to make Lexicon a partner, knowing that the name is a key to their market share. "Our best assignments are when we meet with companies and they lay it all out and together we create a vision," says Placek. Because of its place in the naming-firm food chain, Lexicon more often than not has its pick of clients. Identifying clients that produce good products helps Lexicon tie its reputation to successes, not failures.

The email landscape was an important area when RIM walked in the door. At the time Lexicon was working with RIM, Pitney Bowes, the business communications company, issued a report on workplace communications in the twenty-first century. The report, compiled by the Institute for the Future, a Palo Alto, California–based think tank, painted a picture of a workplace greatly altered by the advent of increasing messages—especially time-delayed messages such as email, faxes, and voice-mail and answering-machine messages. The key points revealed by the study were that messaging has rearranged workdays and redefined productivity, that increased message volume creates more work, and that good communicators send and receive messages strategically. The 1998 study showed that office workers sent and received an average of 190 messages per day. U.S. workers had dramatically shifted their reliance away from real-time or synchronous methods of communication to time-delayed, asynchronous messaging. This is where PocketLink fit in—as a new way to deal with message flow.

In its first stages of creative work, Lexicon immediately moved away from the obvious technological aspects of the device. The namers knew that sticking to strict technology nomenclature would not lead them to an inviting name, one that would appeal to nontechnical consumers. Because the marketers at RIM wanted a wide audience, not just "early adopters" (those consumers who buy any technology when it is fresh), they would seek a name that implied ease of use. The name would have to invite the consumer in—it would have to start the conversation.

Lexicon looks at the early stages of discovery with what it calls a "ship of gold" method. The idea is taken directly from Gary Kinder's book *Ship of Gold in the Deep Blue Sea,* which chronicles the discovery of the SS *Central America,* a gold-laden boat that sank in 1857, two hundred miles off the Carolina coast. To Placek and the team at Lexicon, the most inspiring part of the story is the way Captain Tommy Thompson went about finding the ship's gold—first making a huge sonar sweep of the ocean floor and noting and identifying all the anomalous sunken masses there, and then choosing spots to explore in detail on a second sweep. A wide scan was chosen instead of a probe of every clue. And this is how Lexicon looks at its discovery process, by going wide before narrowing its focus.

RIM Plan of Action

RIM told Lexicon it had about an eighteen-month jump on its competitors in terms of the technology: a critical year and a half to build its brand. Once RIM had signed on, Placek and Hershon created a set of objectives the name would have to communicate. Because the placeholder name, PocketLink, was a qualified descriptive name, Lexicon focused its creative work on connotative names, names that carry implied secondary meanings. Often, Hershon says, clients have invented a placeholder name, and this becomes the one to beat—the one clients keep retreating to, as in, "That one works, but PocketLink is better."

Many creative firms find some sort of academic jargon and

similarly make it their own narrowly defined, in-house shorthand. It can also be a great way to explain heady concepts to clients. Creating a persona for a new product involves linking it to ideas consumers already understand. As Price describes it, every idea in one's head is connected to others—and these ideas form what he calls associative networks. The concept, as used at Lexicon, is based loosely on a premise of cognitive psychology. "We ask ourselves," says Price, "what name or idea will fit into the associative network. But we don't want it to just fit in. We want to know, How can we attach our new idea in a way that will make the associative network *vibrate*? We want people to say 'I get it, *and* it takes me further.' "

The people at Lexicon do not adhere rigidly to the strict definition of an associative network—a way to describe how the mind intuitively comprehends a meaning not yet grasped. It's really a way to envision all of the thoughts in a consumer's head regarding a specific area, whether email tools or hair conditioner.

Lexicon based the RIM project objectives on what it sees as the four components that contribute to a brand name's effectiveness. First, the name must be a vessel capable of carrying a message. Also key are the semantics, phonetics, and sound symbolism associated with the name.

Viewing a brand name as a vessel is fundamental to the Lexicon process, whether the vessel has some meaning already poured into it or stands ready to be filled with meaning that will support an idea, an identity, a personality. This vessel will carry ideas, promises, and buying propositions into the market. "The task is to focus less on whether a name is immediately understood and liked by your customers," Lexicon noted in a list of objectives for RIM, "and to focus more on the name's potential as a vessel to weave an ongoing story that's larger than the brand itself."

At Lexicon, a communications vessel falls along a spectrum running from empty to full. According to Lexicon's standards, there are five categories of names. Words they have created from other words, like *PowerBook, InDesign,* and *LightNote,* are said to be "constructed." Nouns, like *Outback, Forester,* and *Embassy Suites,* are called "real" names. Words that did not exist before, like *Celeron, Pentium,* and *Dasani,* are "invented" terms. Then there are "classical" names, such as *Merus,* and "compressed" names, such as *Optima* (the word *optimal* without the *l*), *Meridia,* and *Industria.*

"It's too hard to go into the market with an almost empty vessel," Placek explains. A word like *PowerBook* is a fuller vessel, because it is composed of two words that have meaning—yet it can still be manipulated to mean other things. A word like *Pentium* is a less full vessel, because it is a made-up word, although the echo of *pent-,* or "five," and the elemental suffix *-ium* serve to fill the vessel. As a word, *Pentium* can be manipulated even more than *PowerBook.* "A brand is a predisposition to buy, a collection of expectations and beliefs," says Placek. "Our mission at Lexicon is to help clients create a vessel that will help them build those predispositions." If a customer comes to a product with a certain leaning, a predisposition, the name supplied by Lexicon should further that leaning, not detract from it.

From a semantic standpoint, the final name needs a literal meaning or set of associations to position the product effectively and communicate a specific idea directly. Lexicon looks beyond the literal meaning of a word or word parts and analyzes other possible associations that the name might suggest.

Phonetically, the structure of a name and its combination of letters affect ease of use, pronunciation, and memorability. Lexicon asks itself whether the name offers a pleasing, rhythmic quality; whether it is constructed to create a balance between vowels and consonants; whether it is likely to be memorable because of its stress patterns; whether it conveys the right tone; and how well it works with any related corporate brands. With consonants (represented by the letter *C*) and vowels *(V)*, the beverage Zima has a prosodic shape. Its CVCV pattern is a universally preferred shape for words in all languages. And the word has to sound right.

Sound symbolism is the study of the relationship between the sound of an utterance and its meaning. Research conducted by Lexicon into the effects of sound symbolism on consumer perception of brand names and whether sounds convey certain ideas shows that in the case of *PowerBook* the initial *P* in *Power* suggests compactness and speed, while the initial *B* in *Book* suggests dependability. Both concepts are important underlying messages for the product.

Consonants called "obstruents" are perceived as harder and more masculine; consonants called "sonorants" are softer and more feminine. *Clorox*—hard-working bleach—has obstruents; the perfume *Chanel* has sonorants. By trying to understand more about how symbolism affects the way people perceive brand names, Lexicon seeks to determine if certain consonant sounds do a better job of communicating specific attributes than others. Linguistic profiles help Lexicon to understand the unique strengths of possible names and to project their performance in the marketplace. For the RIM project, Lexicon noted: "Because the RIM device provides consumers with an easy way to interact with their desktop PC, we will want to communicate sound-symbolically 'easy access' and 'quick response.'"

The objectives Lexicon drew up stipulated that the new name had to support an integrated "new surface" on which to interact with important information when out of the office or away from a desk, that the new name should help deliver a quick, responsive personality, and that it had to be appealing to a broad range of customers—from the on-the-go CEO to the traveling salesperson. Lexicon wrote that because wireless computing technology would make a wide variety of communication services available in the future, the new name should in no way limit the device to email. In their strategic document, Lexicon noted that because the new device is an early entrant into a new category, the new name should help to capture and preempt the new category.

By the time Lexicon was working for RIM, Palm Computing had moved far into the handheld market, to the point that many associated its brand name, *Palm,* with the entire category of proliferating handheld devices. Many people were calling this entire category "palmtop devices" or simply "palms," which was mostly a blessing for Palm Computing. It is hard to say whether this is because Palm Computing was the first handheld computer to attract a wide following, or because the term "palmtop" fits into a taxonomy of desktops and laptops—terms that describe where people use each kind of computer.

Uppercased *Palm* versus lowercased *palm* shows the essence of most trademark disputes. "The ultimate awareness level is brand-named dominance, where, in a recall test, most consumers can provide only the name of a single brand—e.g., A1 Steak Sauce, Kleenex, Xerox, Jell-O," writes David Aaker, author, former business school professor, and one of the more prolific scholars of branding. He goes on, "Ironically, this ultimate success can be tragic if the brand name becomes such a common label for the product that it is not legally protectable. . . . Sometimes it is helpful and even necessary to create a generic name so that the brand does not become one."

Many common nouns—aspirin, cellophane, escalator, nylon—were at one point registered trademarks. Other fairly common words—Coke, Spandex, Dumpster, Velcro, Advil—are still validly registered trademarks, but because of their widespread recognition, one day they could lose their "protect-ability" as trademarks. Many other words stand on this fine line: StairMaster, Popsicle, Ziploc, Muzak, DayGlo. For a company to ensure that it never loses its trademark, it must police its use, and many companies have lawyers who do nothing but this.

As it happens, Palm, the company, was not as vigilant as it could have been early on, when the popularity of its products blossomed. But with a team of lawyers, it sought to use terms like "handheld" at every opportunity, thus framing the category as handhelds—not palms. Palm's lawyers are quick to brush aside any suggestions that its brand name was anywhere close to becoming a generic term. "As the market leader, it is really easy for your product to become synonymous with the product," Jason Firth, Palm's in-house trademark attorney, told me. "There is always danger, but as market leaders you can also influence the lexicography of the industry." Palm has followed a typical course of taking direct legal action against those whom the company sees as abusers of its trademark. Five years after the first Palm Pilot device was launched, Microsoft launched its own PalmPC line—and soon faced a legal challenge from Palm. Having lost the battle, Microsoft now calls its device *PocketPC*. Interestingly, early on, after Pilot Pens filed a lawsuit, Palm lost its use of the trademark *Palm Pilot*—the name under which it launched its first product. Still, in print and in conversation, many people continue to call the device the Palm Pilot.

A repeat client of Lexicon is Procter & Gamble, one of the largest launchers of new products in the world. In the late 1990s, Lexicon created three new names for P&G—*Dryel, Febreze,* and *Swiffer*. All were high-margin products that immediately helped boost P&G's revenues. The team at Lexicon recognized the product that became Swiffer to be more than a mop and more than a broom; it was a totally new kind of device for cleaning the house—an electrostatic duster. P&G wanted to own the category. It was first to market with the new mop, and while the market now hosts similar products from S. C. Johnson (maker of Pledge) and others, its well-named product opened up the category and turned its competitors into copycats. The challenge was not so far from RIM's challenge—P&G needed an archetypal name, and with Swiffer it rapidly created a new product category. Soon, people *swiffed* their floors when they might have *mopped*.

This Just Isn't a Peach or a Banana

When Werezak came back to meet with Lexicon in April 1998, they presented around seventy-five name candidates to him on simple black-and-white cards. He was immediately drawn to the word *blackberry*. Among other things that first went through his mind was the thought "There is no such fruit." In Canada, a blackberry is known as a loganberry, and the idea of a totally fabricated fruit intrigued him. It was a small fruit, he figured, something you could hold your hands.

Werezak also was taken by the symmetry of the name—that *black* and *berry* have five letters each. And he felt that a word ending in *y* was approachable. He liked the playfulness of the name. The color scheme, he knew, fit well with the color of the device.

That said, he withheld his judgment. "We didn't want to get too married to any one name," recalls Werezak, "until the legal process had concluded."

The team at Lexicon had been a big fan of the word *blackberry*, too, none more so than Marc Hershon, who had thought it up. For Lexicon, one initial thought was that the device looked like a strawberry, with its thirty-two-key keyboard reminding them of the pattern and texture of the seeds on a strawberry's surface. "Strawberry, as a word, was too slow," Placek told me. "Blackberry was much faster."

Will Leben is a Stanford University linguistics professor who has consulted for Lexicon since 1989 on sound symbolism, among other linguistics issues. "When you pronounce the word *black*," Leben says, "*black* starts out crisp. The *b* is exploded and the *k* is exploded. These consonants are called 'stops.'" Strawberry, on the other hand, is not a crisp—or fast—word. "*Straw* begins with a hissing sound that goes on a lot longer in time, twice as long as a *b*. The *w* is a vowel sound that also draws out. The *s* sounds lighter and sharper, and the *aw* sounds slower and heavier. It's *ack* versus *aw*."

A few words in any language, says Leben, are onomatopoeic— they come to the language because they imitate the sound they name. In English, think of words like *flip* and *stutter*. But the basic association between sound and meaning is arbitrary. This is the fundamental premise of modern linguistics. When you are creating a word to mean something specific, you can try to harness certain sounds. Leben, in his ongoing consulting role for Lexicon, has worked for a long time to understand the intrinsic meaning of sounds, so they can work to the brand name's advantage. In his role at Lexicon, Leben, in particular, works hard to ensure that the words they create mimic natural language.

Looks are another part of the equation. When one looks at a name, one gets a number of impressions, and linguists systematically sort the jumble. In *BlackBerry*, by capitalizing (or intercapping) the internal *B*, the eye sees that two five-letter words have been put together—and that they are symmetrical. "We also ask, how can we eliminate certain impressions, and accentuate others?" says Leben. The alliteration of *blackberry*, with its two *b*'s, also would help people remember the word.

And, Leben says, he has other linguistic tricks up his sleeve. The most common source of new words is the simple device of metaphor, where one image reminds you of another. Thus, he says, the word *reveal* comes from the French *reveil,* to pull back the veil, a metaphoric image. Using the word *blackberry* for a handheld device makes us think of a small, delicious fruit. Another trick is to use inventive nicknames; as Leben says, "We tend to listen more to ideas when we hear fresh ways to express them." That's why people in New York use *SoHo* to describe the Manhattan neighborhood *so*uth of *Ho*uston Street.

Like Apple Computer, *blackberry* is friendly, says Leben: "A blackberry is something you like, and you are not intimidated by. It's delicious, and it's special—you find them and you think, 'How nice.' It's an everyday object, with pleasant connotations. It has good connotations of the familiar and the special." This semantic component, that blackberries are approachable, easy-to-pick fruit, would help BlackBerry bring positive associations to its category instantly. And it's worth noting that in some ways BlackBerry is derivative of Apple Computer—limning the connotations of that brand into its own.

In his report, Leben also looked at the familiarity of the component words and what they convey. *Black, berry,* and *blackberry* are all words that we know, Leben points out. "Compare Black-Berry with a more literal device, say Command Port, and you can feel the difference." BlackBerry, says Leben, implicitly says to you that you won't have to read a two-hundred-page manual.

After Werezak checked out the list of name candidates, he invited Placek and Hershon to his firm's headquarters to show it to the RIM executive team, including founder Mike Lazaridis and co-CEO Jim Balsillie, who had joined in 1992 as a high-energy financial whiz to complement Laziridis's more relaxed technological genius. At the meeting, the advance team from Lexicon chose first to present around forty names to the group at RIM, so it would see the history of the project. "Sometimes if you just show five names, a client does not understand the amount of work that has gone on," says Placek, who must in some sense sell the names to his clients. Gaining consensus, after all, is also a part of his job.

At the presentation, Lexicon told a group of high-level Research In Motion staff and executives that, first and foremost, they would *not* like 10 percent of the names, and that they *would* like 10 percent. The percentages come from Lexicon's experience with hundreds of client engagements. Lexicon also pointed out that they could learn a lot from the remaining 80 percent.

The team was then given decks of thick card stock, which Placek says "makes the names feel substantive." The following words each took a page: *AirWire, Badge, Banjo, Banter, BlackBerry, Cera, Cielo, Combio, ComTop, Cyphra, Dyrex, eBox, eTop, Evex, GamePlan, Geode, Grip, Hula, IntraTop, LiveRide, Mica, Mini-Top, Nemo, OutRigger, Photon, Pouch, Reon, Riff, Ryto, Slide, Sling, Tailwind, Tecton, TelTop, Transilion, Transite, Veon, Verb, Vion, Vuant, Waterfall, Wheels,* and *WorldTop.*

Although the group would have difficulty seeing it at the time, just glancing at this list now makes it as clear as daylight that BlackBerry was the best choice. It would "support an integrated 'new surface'"; it would appeal to a broad range of customers "from the on-the-go CEO to the traveling salesperson"; it "would deliver a quick, responsive personality"; it would not "limit the device to email"; and the brand would carry the "expectations, beliefs, and promises [of] interactive access, integrated communication, convenient, wireless, portable, personal, and vital." Out of the forty-three finalists, it was the only one that really met most of the original criteria.

"We want to give people a new way to think about what they are doing," says Placek. "And BlackBerry was a great way to do that. I mean, this just isn't a peach or a banana. People could visualize a blackberry network growing on the vine."

Although Werezak was the point man on the naming project, he did not have the final say in the naming decision. As it turned out, the rest of the executive team, including President Mike Lazaridis, had quite a lot to say. At the presentation, Lexicon was surprised by the candid way that Lazaridis, Balsillie, and Werezak spoke with one another. Werezak, for his part, stood as a champion of the name BlackBerry, and spoke frankly with his colleagues about its values.

They knew choosing a connotative name—like *BlackBerry*—would mean a larger investment on their part, but they also knew it was important to do so. *BlackBerry*, as a word, would not immediately make people think of the exact product they had for sale. Advertising dollars would have to be spent to link the word with the product. Werezak might have known what *connotative* meant when he first met with Lexicon, but by the end of the process it was hardwired into his vocabulary. "We had branded our interactive pager line the 900 line," recalled Werezak. "BlackBerry was going to be a bigger investment for us because of what it takes to go with a connotative name." The major upside, he noted: "It's hard to copy and confuse anything with BlackBerry."

From BlackBerry to CrackBerry

RIM launched the BlackBerry in January 1999 and initially relied on a grassroots-oriented marketing campaign to get its message out. Among other things, email sent from a BlackBerry has a signature that says, "Sent from my BlackBerry Wireless Handheld." This was a lot like Hotmail email, which told recipients that they, too, could get free email by signing up with Hotmail. ("Viral marketing" is what Hotmail calls it, the effect of one email user spreading a message exponentially.) In February 2000, *Forbes* named BlackBerry one of seven "cult brands," along with Ben & Jerry's and Nike. In April 2000, RIM launched its first national advertising and branding campaign for BlackBerry, with a tag line of "Berry Berry Productive," which served to increase dramatically the awareness and recognition of BlackBerry in the corporate computing market. Meanwhile, the product was getting numerous awards, like the World Class Award for Best Wireless Communication Device from *PC World Magazine* for its small and lightweight design and constant access to email. The BlackBerry helped raise RIM's annual revenue to $294 million in 2002 (up from $8.7 million in 1997).

The BlackBerry found its way into executive suites all over the country. And not only executives used them—senators, baseball players, and movie stars got them, too. Nerdy Al Gore was an early adopter, as were many in his failed 2000 presidential campaign. After the September 11 terrorist attacks, more than one member of the United States Congress found the BlackBerry effective for communicating at a time of overloaded cell phone networks. The Committee on House Administration soon ordered 435 BlackBerries for House members, and eventually bought upwards of three thousand of the devices and invested $6 million in the technology.

Some joked about the addictive nature of the tiny, ubiquitous "CrackBerry." Although most of its customers were in the corporate market, RIM inked more deals with consumer-oriented organizations such as AOL and Yahoo! to bring in new noncorporate clients. Nokia, at the same time, had launched a phone-and-email device called the Nokia Communicator. Based on the size of the device, many came to call it "the Brick." Nokia tried to fight this, but with little success.

Even as the BlackBerry received more and more recognition, it faced encroachments from Motorola, Handspring, and Palm, companies with much higher visibility in the consumer market. In a 2001 magazine article, co-CEO Jim Balsillie framed the company's prospects as a battle of the beasts. "Who wins between an alligator and a bear?" he asked. "It all depends on the terrain—do they fight on water, land, or mud? So it goes with wireless."

RIM's 2001 annual report was awash in BlackBerry. I wondered whether the word would soon take over the corporate name, Research In Motion. The company doubled its workforce from eight hundred in early 2000 to more than 1,600 in mid-2002. During the summer of 2002, RIM opened a second manufacturing plant, so it could produce up to 6 million of the BlackBerry and other computing devices per year, up from 1 million in 2001. In mid-2002, some 320,000 people were using the BlackBerry at more than 14,500 organizations. BlackBerry was catching on.

Distilling Stories

Most naming firms have a handful of words that constantly come up during creative projects and brainstorms—a virtual file folder of words they know will someday apply to some client. The name "Monorail" had been floating around since the mid-1990s, when the Gap rejected it for its chain of low-priced clothing stores. It surfaced in 1997 attached to a company operating as a reseller of computers. Same namer.

BlackBerry was one of those names kicking around a naming firm, looking for a home. I had heard it brought up in a creative session years before. My notes from my very first day as a namer contain the word *blackberry*. Someone built on the notion of a blackberry as a network and mentioned the word *tendrils*. I even wrote about this when I published my article on naming in *Wired*, more than a year before BlackBerry was named.

So, after the reporting I had done, and extensive interviews with Placek and Company, I was left to ponder. Was all the talk about "divergent thinking" voiced by Placek, convincing as he is, undercut by the appearance of the word years before? Placek did not want to comment. I wondered whether everything Lexicon had told me about the suitability of the word to RIM had been hocus-pocus. Or was it really all about the story Lexicon told me, and the story it told RIM, and then the story RIM told its customers and the press? Maybe Lexicon had created a word and found a client for which it really was the best match.

David Placek's mastery is in working with clients to give the impression that their product is niche-defining, even if it is not. Zima (the Russian word for winter) was not just beer, it was a *clearmalt beverage*. Pentium was not just another chip, it was an *Intel processor*. Slates were not just pants, but *dress slacks*. BlackBerry would similarly succeed through claiming its own niche. When you go to a company like Lexicon, you take away more than just a name; you are indoctrinated into a new story—a story you will tell your customers and they will tell one another. A good brand name spreads with a good story, and the initial tellers of the story are critical to its success. The people at Lexicon help you tell the story. And the story they have about themselves is just as important as the list of names they have produced in the past. If a naming firm doesn't have a good story to tell you about its own process—its philosophy, its spin—then how can you expect it to help you?

One way to demonstrate this is by reviewing the list of objectives Lexicon laid out at the project's outset. The name *BlackBerry* (a fruit that grows on vines) did in fact help to support the notion of a link to the office or desk; it is appealing to a broad range of customers; it has a "quick personality," as they called it; and it does not limit the device to email (although that's what it's best known for at present). The brand does carry the stated expectations, beliefs, and promises: interactive access, integrated communication, convenient, wireless, portable, personal, and vital. And the new name has captured its own category of wireless email solutions fairly well. Just a few years after its launch, the word was fully part of the business press vernacular: A *New York Times* lead paragraph wrote of stock analysts racing out of a Merck press conference and "feverishly contacting their trading desks on their cell phones and BlackBerries to report a bombshell for investors." BlackBerry had truly arrived.

In March 2002, RIM announced its BlackBerry 5810—an email device that was also a phone. "The convergence of voice and data is just beginning," Werezak told me. In May 2002, an upstart company called Good Technology introduced a knockoff called GoodLink that might yet give BlackBerry a run for its money. BlackBerry likely will remain a niche product for power email users, and it will face much competition in the years ahead. Still, its name had worked well, considering the competition. "We can make a difference in an odd way," Placek says. "Most marketers don't give much thought to the name. BlackBerry helped RIM create a set of expectations and beliefs—which is what a brand is at Lexicon. The name can unlock the power of the product. *BlackBerry* unlocked the power of this device."

What was once PocketLink was effectively rechristened BlackBerry—a name that much better mimicked natural, organic language than did PocketLink. And the word was not a coined word but a real word that people already had positive associations with. BlackBerry reflected natural language patterns; it was not an awkward hybrid. Like Saturn, which once made one think of the planet with rings, not an economically priced American car, BlackBerry had hacked its own new meaning out of the public consciousness.

MAVERICK
THINKING

4

In 1845, Samuel Maverick was presented with four hundred head of cattle in lieu of a payment of $1,200 for land he sold in Texas. He did not take much of an interest in the beasts or in the work of raising cattle. Nevertheless, Maverick's legacy as a cattleman lives on.

Maverick let the cattle roam free and unbranded under the supervision of a family that managed his property on Matagorda Bay, on the Gulf Coast of Texas, and then in Conquista, on the east bank of the San Antonio River. The cattle were left "to graze, to fatten, to multiply and to wander away," in the words of Maverick's son George, who wrote about the herd forty years later. That the cows wandered was not a big deal, but that Maverick failed to brand the majority of the cattle with his insignia—as was the standard procedure—meant they were viewed as free and ownerless, unmarked stock. Why Maverick did not brand his cattle is still not really understood. He simply may have been lazy.

The branding of cattle, an ancient practice popularized in the western United States in the 1800s, allowed owners to let their herds mingle on the open plains, while still maintaining ownership. Because Maverick's cattle had no ornamentation—no brand—that proved his ownership, his neighbors came to call all wandering, unbranded cattle "Maverick's"; later the word was applied to any unbranded animal on the range.

As the name and the story of Samuel Maverick's unbranded herd came to be told across the western frontier of the United States, the issue of ownership became complex. There were those who believed that because Maverick failed to brand his cattle, he could essentially count any unbranded cattle he found as his own. This included calves born during the winter. In this line of thinking, Maverick comes off as a passive cattle rustler. And indeed, as legend has it, he subsequently became the largest cattle owner in Texas.

It fell to his heirs (who were saddled with his name and all of its interpretations) to defend the herd and prove that in fact, having not branded his cattle, Maverick slowly lost his herd to cowboys who took the opportunity to mark the unbranded, unclaimed cattle. His son George said that the neighbors easily assumed ownership of Maverick's herd simply by heating up their own branding irons and burning "into [the cows'] tender hides their own brands, [so] the beasts were Maverick's ('mavericks') no longer."

As George Maverick wrote of his father's legacy: "If unbranded who is the owner? Who can tell? It becomes impossible to decide the question of ownership, but right here one thing does happen—the unbranded beast adopts a name and is known as a 'maverick'—meaning 'nobody's calf.' "

On the face of it, an act like Maverick's, launching unprotected assets into the world, might not seem to be a good business decision. But that is in fact what some sophisticated marketers have done, with increasing success, in recent years.

The story of Maverick and his cattle bridges the gap between old and new brands. Just as branding cattle predominated in Texas in the 1800s, rigid legal trademarking of goods and services is the standard procedure today. But in the verbal branding arena, where, by talking about brands by using specific words, people can increase the value of the brands—some call this "talk value"—strict legal adherence is not always the best option. If talk is hampered, words will not spread. The freedom with which Maverick's unbranded cows traveled is the chief reason for the spread of the idea of a *maverick* cow. We don't usually think of language as free or owned, but this is a major conceit of trademark law, under which all brand names fall.

From Brand to Branded

In the transformation of every brand name—from brand name to brand—a trajectory occurs that is akin to that evolution of Maverick from surname to shorthand. A brand name comes to represent more than just a word.

Hugh Dubberly, an interaction designer, studies how people relate to information and designs systems to facilitate enhanced interactions. He devised a model that charts people's interactions with brands: from the first point of interaction, into experience, and the shaping of a perception. First a customer experiences the product in some manner—either by viewing an ad, by seeing the product in a store, or by actually using it. That *experience* shapes an idea in the mind—and that idea floating in the mind *is* the brand. The brand links the experience you have to the idea in your mind.

Dubberly worked at Apple Computer for a few years, and he uses the Apple brand to explain his model. Apple makes a lot of products, the most famous of which is the Macintosh. A person who knows about Apple might know about these products, and he or she might have some knowledge of Apple CEO Steve Jobs. The person might have some past experience with an Apple computer, the typeface of its ads, and its industrial design. The person might have a feeling about Microsoft and the Windows Operating System, and how these competitively relate to Apple. "You tie all those things together in your mind. The brand is an aggregate of what is in your mind and everybody else's minds."

"There is a set of people who all know German—it lives in their mind," says Dubberly. The official rules that govern the German language exist in books, but people carry the living language. Similarly, Apple—and everything about Apple—exists in people's minds. "My friends at Apple are responsible for the brand, but really the brand does not live at Apple. It is what you think of Apple." The people responsible for a brand, in Dubberly's model, are *brand stewards*. The stewards, Dubberly points out, "can't actually make the experience, they can only make artifacts and services. The experience is something that you have with the artifacts and services. The experience lives with the consumer, it is made by the consumer." One of the primary artifacts is the name. Call it artifact number one.

As I met more of the people involved in naming things, I quickly found myself adrift in a world with its own jargon surrounding brands, branding, and brand names. The way David Placek explained Lexicon's role was that his firm made brand names and his clients built brands with those names. But few, aside from Placek, wanted to be known as simply namers—"We do brand strategy here," I was told, "We build brands," or "We are corporate storytellers." There are many definitions because definitions are propagated by branding "experts," consultants, and writers, whose livelihood depends on their own specific definition being right. There is an industry-wide vagueness and reluctance to nail down just exactly what a brand is, because each person wants to be the authority. The truth is that there is no correct answer to what a brand is. The books that proliferate on the subject all define brands and branding in slightly different terms.

The most common marketing definition of a brand is that it is a *promise*—an unspoken pact between a company and a consumer to deliver a particular experience. Some strategists examine the brand experience (what Starbucks is best known for), some look at emotional branding (Nike), some look at differentiating the brand (Chiquita), some talk of living the brand (Martha Stewart Living, at least before the insider-trading scandal), some talk of brand loyalty (Volvo), some talk of brand awareness (Coca-Cola). All the talk of megabrands, powerbranding, and building brands are variations on the basic equation—encounter, experience, idea—that Dubberly describes in his model.

To those who trumpet the power of the brand over all, its cornerstone, the name, represents huge amounts of money to its owner. A company with a big-time brand—think McDonald's, Adidas, Toyota—could burn its factories and lay off its staff, but if, at the end of the day, the brand remained, this most valuable commodity would allow the company to soldier on. At its most extreme, things like manufacturing excellence and enduring profitable growth are discounted in the face of the almighty brand.

Some consider the 1988 sale of Kraft for $13 billion to Philip Morris as a turning point in the history of brands, after which the value of a brand name was no longer abstract, but calculable as a corporate asset. To many, the sale did not focus on the tangible aspects of Kraft the company, such as its products, staff, management, and physical property. Instead, for a price 600 percent over its book value, Philip Morris bought the intangible corporate image or brand—all of the qualities that consumers had come to associate with the name "Kraft" and that encourage consumers to pay a premium for products that seem nearly identical to cheaper alternatives. The name "Kraft" alone is enough to make consumers buy, and Philip Morris was willing to pay a lot of money for it.

As I got in deeper I had to fashion my own working definition of what a brand is to make sense of the world I had entered. It is a fluid word, the verbal equivalent of quicksand. To me this was part of the fascination—everywhere I turned, I found another way to define the very word that was hanging in the background of my entire etymological endeavor.

To me, a brand is an amalgamation of everything that one thinks about when a particular word is uttered, and an encapsulated message is called forth. When someone says Amazon, I usually think about the large Web retailer based in Seattle before I think of the South American drainage where more than 40 percent of the earth's fresh water flows. I think about getting a cardboard box in the mail that's filled with books (and the meeting I had at Amazon's ad agency where a creative director briefed me about the "joy of opening the box from Amazon"). I think about how *Time* magazine awarded Amazon CEO Jeff Bezos its "Person of the Year" award in 1999. And I think about the *Fortune* magazine billboard with Bezos's face on it near my house in San Francicso that read cryptically, "In the land of the blind, the one-eyed man is king." The billboard was up for months, growing tattered and faded as the Internet boom turned to bust.

The point here is that Amazon, that one word, summons a great deal of images and ideas in my head. It is all these things that come subsequent to a name that make a *brand name* a *brand*. The name is the launch pad, the foundation for building the brand. And anyone involved in a branding process works to ensure that the thoughts that customers or possible customers call up in their mental databanks are positive.

To follow the word *brand* back in time is to first see brand defined as a burning stick, a fire-warmed poker. Later, it is the mark made by burning with a hot iron, a definition indicating mark of ownership, used in the branding of animals—searing their hides with a mark. Later still, it becomes a brand-mark or what we now think of as a trademark, a mark that indicates a guarantee of quality for customers. In the mid-twentieth century, the terms *brand-image* and *brand name* emerged, first attributed to adman David Ogilvy and defined as the impression of a product in the minds of potential users or consumers, the set of associations and experiences that are more than the mark and the name. Throughout history, brands have maintained two defining characteristics—one of ownership, and one of dissemination. To send out a new word into the world of commerce involves first owning the word (an increasingly difficult proposition) and then effectively propagating the word (also no easy feat).

ACCENTURE
ADAPTS TO THE
FUTURE

5

It was a classic teaser campaign, and I was being teased. The ads turned up in the hallways between airplane departure gates frequented by business travelers, on billboards in financial districts, in magazines like *Forbes* and *Fortune* that businesspeople make a habit of reading, in the kinds of places where businesspeople find themselves when they are not in front of computers.

The idea behind the tease was simple: to engage me and enroll me in an unfolding corporate name change narrative. And the tease went like this: "Renamed. Redefined. Reborn. 01.01.01" and "Now it gets interesting." As someone tracking new words, I followed the trail to Andersen Consulting to find out why it was changing its name, where this company had come from, and just how it had come up with its new, *interesting* name.

Global brand launches—from scratch—are pretty rare. Most large brands have some background, some history, something to build and expand on. The name Andersen Consulting drew a straight line from distinguished origins—those of its founder, Arthur Andersen, an astute accountant who first worked at Price,

Waterhouse. In 1913, with partner Clarence Delany, he started his own firm: Andersen, Delany, & Company, which in 1918 became simply Arthur Andersen & Company. For the next eighty-plus years the company grew, to become a giant company named Andersen Worldwide—one of the largest professional services firms in the world, and the biggest of the Big Six accounting firms—that oversaw two sister companies, Arthur Andersen and Andersen Consulting. But in August 2000, the lineage of Arthur Andersen was severed forever.

As Arthur Andersen grew his firm in the 1920s, he was guided by a strong principle that clients would turn to his people for their accounting needs because his firm would offer consistent advice and never contradict itself. "If we fail to speak consistently with one voice," he said, "we will confuse clients and undermine the credibility that is crucial to an auditor's success." Andersen himself ran the company for a number of years, always wearing a yellow rose in his lapel, a floral representation of his singular voice. The impeccable reputation he had built, and the size and scope of the firm itself, continued to grow after his death in 1947.

One of the more successful areas to bloom within the Arthur Andersen organization was a division that eventually came to be known as Andersen Consulting. This group—launched in 1942 as Administrative Accounting—looked into the development of systems, methods, and procedures throughout the firm. In 1951, it was renamed the Administrative Services Division and became the Management Information Consulting Division, or MICD, in 1980. In 1989, this MICD group was rechristened Andersen Consulting, and its business operations were separated from sibling Arthur Andersen, a group that was composed chiefly of accountants.

The division that became Andersen Consulting was filled with consultants who came to offer expert advice on key issues faced by top executives at client companies. What had started as a minor department grew quickly and soon generated revenue that outpaced the accounting division's receipts. As Andersen built up its consulting practice, the consultants and the accountants at the firm slowly split into factions. Despite more than a few attempts to close the growing rift, a schism grew between the accountant bean counters and the consultant suits. The revenue inequality and growing differences between the people in the two divisions drove a wedge into the company. In 1977, the firm tried to heal the rift by structurally maintaining the one-firm concept with Andersen Worldwide in charge. But the one voice that had long prevailed at Arthur Andersen & Company slowly, painfully, became two quarreling ones.

Business had changed. By the 1980s, following the reengineering that had swept corporate America, management consulting was an emblematic component of the world of business. More and more companies turned to consultants like Andersen to streamline processes, to make their companies run better, and to cut costs by justifying, through their expert (and high-priced) recommendations, the firing of workers and other cost-cutting measures. This shift in the global economy meant that consultants were worth more—and could charge more—than accountants.

By the early 1990s, management-consulting firms attracted the best and brightest workers. Andersen and its competitors recruited heavily on the campuses of elite colleges, and siphoned off talent in droves. Consulting became a goal for many graduating seniors. By making the consulting firms *seem* like destinations for the best graduates, they became just that. In 1998 alone, Andersen Consulting hired almost sixteen thousand consultants. Fat paychecks, solid training, and intellectually challenging positions made up for the inconvenience of almost constant travel to client sites. Still, the work was grueling enough to keep turnover rates as high as 15 percent.

Management consultants are similar to branding consultants in that they operate as outside teams that offer external modes of problem solving. Unlike tiny consulting firms such as Lexicon, information technology implementers like IBM and Andersen and the big strategy firms—Bain & Company, Boston Consulting Group, McKinsey & Company, Booz Allen, Monitor, Marakon Associates, and Mercer—try to keep the creative side of consulting alive through rigid systematic means, as opposed to constantly adapting their models to suit new clients. Andersen's selling point has long been that it takes a client from a strategy phase through actual implementation of the strategy—whether it is a new computer system or a company-wide shakeup. The firm is involved in computer systems integration, hardware configuration, and operation training for clients. In 2002, company clients included seventy-nine of the Fortune 100 companies in the United States, and nearly two-thirds of the Fortune Global 500.

Because of their growing relevance in solving problems for clients, the management consultants continued to clash internally with the accountants. In 1990, the sibling companies tried again to rectify growing disparities between their units. In an agreement that came to be known as the Florida Accords, the two siblings and their parent company sought to ameliorate their differences by acknowledging that even though each business unit competed with the other in some ways, together their strategies had to fit within an overall firm strategy. Implementing this ideal grew more difficult as Arthur Andersen ramped up its own consulting division. The temporary patch lasted about a decade and included a stipulation that each year the more profitable of the two sister firms would have to pay part of its revenue to the less profitable firm, an amount that was capped at 15 percent.

All Andersen companies were run as privately held partnerships, so the partners who ran each division had a real stake in where the revenues went. Aside from the differences in personality between the accountants and consultants, there was a feeling among the consultants that they were increasingly paying their sister and parent company more than a fair share of revenues as part of the Florida Accords.

As managing partner, George Shaheen led Andersen Consulting through this divisive period, and under his leadership Andersen Consulting's revenues grew from $1.4 billion in 1989 to $9.6 billion in 1999. Things finally came to a head when, in December 1997, Shaheen voiced a novel idea—that Andersen Consulting should spin off and away from its parent to become a free agent, a stand-alone company. The company formally filed a request to separate. It was a bold move that precipitated a long legal battle and pitted the two sibling firms against each other for more than two and a half years. As the battle began, it was clear that the name of each firm might come to be the central issue in any negotiated settlement.

One Voice Becomes Two

Two companies that made their living by solving the problems of other organizations now were unable to solve their own. The battle threatened to sprawl into complete public view until both firms, realizing the futility of bashing each other in the press, reached a gentlemen's agreement. Andersen Consulting, as the "claimants," turned to the Paris-based International Court of Arbitration of the International Chamber of Commerce (ICC) to help settle the growing dispute. Through ICC they found an arbitrator based in Colombia, one of the few countries in which neither firm operated. The essence of the dispute centered around the 1990 Florida Accords, in which they had essentially split up their duties—Andersen Consulting would consult and Arthur Andersen would audit (except for some smaller consulting projects). Andersen Consulting charged that Arthur Andersen had in fact become involved in consulting with larger companies valued at more than $175 million, in violation of the Florida agreement.

As the two firms headed for a split in 1999, each wanted to gain something in the divorce. For its part, Arthur Andersen wanted Andersen Consulting to pay $14.6 billion for breaking contractual obligations, a payment they arrived at by calculating 150 percent of Andersen Consulting's 1999 revenues. Arthur Andersen wanted Andersen Consulting to forsake its name and the shared technology it regarded as its own. Andersen Consulting sought to give up no technologies, pay no exit fee, keep its name, and become independent.

Lawyers for Andersen Consulting called Kevin Keller, a marketing professor at Dartmouth's Tuck School of Business, to defend its claim on the Andersen name. Keller's expert report claimed that Andersen Consulting had made substantial investments in the name "Andersen Consulting." Because Arthur Andersen wanted Andersen Consulting to relinquish its name, Keller sought to show that in its nine years of existence, Andersen Consulting had created the majority of brand value for its name—*Andersen Consulting*—through its own efforts. Keller sent in a paper detailing the value of the name *Andersen* to Andersen Consulting. By comparing the brand name with others and examining how consumers perceived the words, he valued the name at around $7 billion, implying that taking away the name would be a major loss to the company.

The final award pointed out that "[i]n 1993 Mr. Shaheen proclaimed 'When Andersen Consulting faced the dilemma of creating its own image in the marketplace, we paid careful consideration to our name. From our research and discussions, and plain gut instinct, it became apparent that we would never want to change from the Andersen name.' It was obvious to Mr. Shaheen that the reputation of Arthur Andersen had been built by the men and women who had preceded the actual partners over seventy-five years."

The *Andersen* arbitration was, in essence, "a global divorce proceeding of the most extraordinary proportions," wrote reviewers of the case in an industry journal. After almost a year of deliberation, ICC judge Gilberto Gamba handed down his ruling on August 7, 2000. Andersen Worldwide was found to have breached obligations to its daughter companies by not sticking to previous operating agreements, but Arthur Andersen had not breached obligations. Andersen Consulting was released from all contractual obligations and did not have to pay any money to Arthur Andersen. But it had to relinquish its name by the end of the year (in 147 days) to Arthur Andersen, which would retain legal title to the name. All in all, the various parties in the ICC arbitration spent more than $45 million defending themselves.

Both sides claimed victory and remained in disagreement. "This is very significant, because the value of an organization is its reputation, its people, and its brand. The value of the brand is not in the word 'Arthur' or the word 'consulting,' it's in the name 'Andersen,'" Arthur Andersen's then-chief executive Jim Wadia said after the ruling. He resigned four hours after the announcement.

The stripping of Andersen Consulting's name represented the transfer of a highly valuable commodity. Yet in many ways the ruling was a victory for Andersen Consulting, which did not have to pay the $14.6 billion Arthur Andersen wanted—an amount that would have crippled the company.

The ruling set in motion a high-speed, multimillion-dollar global chase for a new identity. It was a chance to turn adversity into a successful rebranding campaign to show off to prospective clients. Paying $14 billion would have been life-threatening; changing a name was just immensely challenging. Andersen Consulting spun the decision as a victory and celebrated its newfound freedom from both its parent company and its sibling, publicly treating its own renaming as a simple baptism, not the baptism by fire it really was.

Now It Gets Interesting

Teresa Poggenpohl was a perfect person to lead the name-creation push of the company's rebranding effort. Poggenpohl was pretty much an Andersen Consulting lifer. After getting her MBA at the University of Illinois in 1986, she went to work for Arthur Andersen and watched as, two years later, the parent firm spun off her division and named it Andersen Consulting, which she felt was a logical if dull name choice. She went to London to manage the overseas branding office of the developing Andersen Consulting.

The notion of corporate branding was a fresh one at the time, even more so in the consulting world. Poggenpohl, though young and inexperienced, found herself with a strong role in the new company's marketing division. By 2000, she had been named a partner at Andersen and director of global advertising research and brand management. Poggenpohl, at forty-two, has preppy good looks, straight brown hair she wears in a bob, and a fondness for pearl earrings. She has the pragmatic sensibilities of someone who might walk to work in running shoes.

After the court handed down its judgment, Andersen chief executive Joe Forehand was quick to add $100 million to Poggenpohl's budget to oversee the name change and rebranding effort.

A day after hearing the ruling, Poggenpohl called a meeting of the forty or so people who were to become key members of the re-branding team. Among this group was Tom Pollan, who directed the nuts and bolts of the project by leading the program management office. This group would be responsible for everything from changing the signage on 178 Andersen Consulting facilities worldwide to reprinting more than 65,000 sets of business cards. Representatives of Andersen's advertising agency, Young & Rubicam, and its branding agency, Landor Associates, also joined the meeting. In a highly charged and enthusiastic gathering, the group succinctly laid out the rebranding plan.

As part of the court-mandated name change, team members knew they had limited time to deliver. They needed a new name by January 1, 2001—just 147 days away. Thereafter they would have a mere ninety days to even refer to the old name. The company would have to molt like a reptile—shed its identity in a period of metamorphoses and emerge anew.

Initially the newly named company would want clients to recognize that the new company was the old company. Then, over time, clients would ideally not associate the two at all—and the new firm would cut loose from the old. The equity of the old name would have to be transferred into the new name, and then the new name would have to gain global awareness. "It's delicate; on the one hand you want to make the connection to the old company, and on the other hand you want to say, 'But we are more, we are something new that you probably haven't thought of,'" recalled Poggenpohl.

Before the initial meeting had progressed very far, someone suggested they hire a video crew to record that gathering—and every subsequent one. They were making history, after all, and what's more, they would have documentary evidence to show future clients. The crew, directed by Charles Teeter, a manager of the global brand team, went on to shoot more than one hundred hours of tape during the 147 critical days leading up to January 1. Teeter also bought a number of handheld video cameras that he fedexed around the world at critical times to capture important meetings, what he calls "videograbs."

The hours and hours of tape chronicle Andersen Consulting and its various outsourced assistants slowly but surely traversing the path to a new name. Because I was not there, these videotapes served as my own personal tour of the rebranding process. Most of the tapes are filled with businesspeople dressed casually at meetings in various well-appointed office spaces and corporate conference sites in Florida. Not surprisingly, owing to the company's culture of efficiency and event planning, there is little evidence of chaos. Nonscripted events were, presumably, erased from the public record.

The story largely wrote itself, but true to Andersen Consulting standards, Teeter outlined most of the story before it played out. The only real surprise would be who created the final name. The team worked backward to write a script that covered three key areas: the history, the rebranding process and associated strategy; the act of bringing the brand to life; and the launch. The eventual audience included people at Andersen as well as clients and members of the media.

Because the rebranding effort necessitated vast coordination and program management, Poggenpohl became a client of her own people who managed the complex undertaking, with twenty-five Andersen consultants dedicated to the task of identifying milestones and tracking forward motion.

Luckily, Poggenpohl and her department already had begun to rebrand the firm before the judge's orders were handed down. Since Andersen Consulting had split off from Arthur Andersen in 1989, they had worked with outside vendor Landor Associates on branding issues. Landor had executed Andersen Consulting's first brand identity as well as a subsequent tweak—and Landor was working on a third before the name change was mandated. During the previous update of the brand, Landor had created a new logo that looked like an *A* with a superscript *C* to the right of it— *A* to the *C*. It was somehow math-related, but fairly unclear.

Poggenpohl's group also had in place some two thousand so-called brand champions: employees spread all over the world, most of whom worked in marketing departments in various global locations. That group, having helped to promote the importance of the corporate identity before, was called up like a reservist army to inspire the company about the rebranding project and to build consensus around a new name.

When the name change project was launched, Andersen Consulting was engaged in an in-depth reexamination of its business strategies. The executive team, led by Forehand (who became managing partner in November 1999), was already openly questioning the descriptor "consulting." This initiative was actually driven by Poggenpohl's group, which sought to change the brand image every three to five years. While standard brand strategy indicates that such frequent change might detract from or dilute a brand, Poggenpohl says that in business-to-business and technology consulting, "Change is the ethos. You have to push the envelope." Change is also the product that Andersen sells to its clients—the company must show that it embraces and practices change to sell it enthusiastically and effectively.

Andersen Consulting is the kind of company that works overtime to claim that it does not have a headquarters—a way, perhaps, to come across as a more even-keeled place where the location one happens to work in is less important than the fact that one is part of a large partnership. (And perhaps to keep the troops intent on becoming partners themselves.) This is also a way to reach clients all over the world. This notion started under the watch of managing partner George Shaheen, who called Andersen Consulting a global entity. In point of fact, most of the employees lived and worked in Chicago or nearby, where Arthur Andersen launched his firm long ago. With its new name in place, the company once known as Andersen Consulting showed no mention of the Andersen legacy on its Web-based corporate history. It established financial headquarters in Switzerland, a holding company in Luxembourg, and a parent company in Bermuda, and disavowed its American lineage entirely.

Like other old-line companies in the mid-1990s, Andersen Consulting struggled a bit with its identity—trying to make itself relevant and interesting to the recent college graduates it had once so easily hired but who lately were heading in droves to more sexy Internet startup companies. The dot-com boom made the company feel like a dinosaur. It decided that, among other things, it wanted to be known as a "bridge builder," whatever that meant.

The company decided to make the search for a new name into an internal contest. With some 65,000 employees, this would greatly expand the quest. Gary Beckner had never managed such a wide-reaching project, but as head of Andersen's Global Events and Special Projects team he was appointed to launch the in-house competition, an effort he and his group dubbed, not entirely originally, "brandstorming." The contest served two purposes—to try to elicit a winning name internally, and also to start to build a consensus within the sprawling organization around the idea of a name change. A memo went out from Jim Murphy, Andersen's marketing head, dated August 22, 2000, titled "Help rename the firm and win a trip to Australia."

After the ICC ruling in August 2000, Poggenpohl and her team immediately began to think about what kind of a name they wanted to create. They knew that they wanted an umbrella-like, all-encompassing name—a vessel that was more empty than it was full. Expansive and synthetic names were increasingly popular among large corporations that wanted to infuse their name with more meaning as it grew—and not to be weighed down by specifics (like the word "consulting").

Most names have a limit to how far you can stretch them—or fill them with meaning. The typical brand name can be seen as a "rubber band," say brand strategy authors Al Ries and Jack Trout. They write that such a name "will stretch, but not beyond a certain point . . . The more you stretch a name, the weaker it becomes." But an umbrella name is stretchable. And stretched, synthetic names also happen to be a lot easier for people to agree on because they represent a lowest common denominator. Not a consensus builder, but a consensus destination. If a name means little, it likely will not offend anyone.

Poggenpohl wanted the name to follow a standard branding construct and be "aspirational" as well. "You had to think of Andersen Consulting on its best day and describe that—the best partner on the best day, that's what you had to aspire to," she says. With this aspirational model in place, you communicate the company's dream internally and externally.

Andersen turned to its longtime partner Landor Associates, a pioneer in the field of branding, to create the new name and to lead and manage its corporate identity change.

For Landor, the project differed from typical jobs in several ways. For legal reasons, the deadline could not be missed. The legal mandate to stop using the Andersen name after ninety days required special PR efforts by Burson-Marsteller and advertising help from Young & Rubicam, both Landor sister companies under the WPP umbrella. To meet the fixed deadline, many steps that ideally would have been taken sequentially were instead executed concurrently. Because Andersen operated in more than forty countries, more names were developed and screened for trademark infringement and for native speaker and marketplace appropriateness (in sixty-five languages) than for any other naming project Landor had conducted. Andersen's business spanned at least seven international trademark classes, and this made clearance of the trademark an especially formidable hurdle.

The Medium Is the Message

Many consider Walter Landor to be the father of corporate identity. Born in 1913 and raised in Germany, Landor found influences in the Werkbund, an industrial federation that sought to raise manufacturing standards, and the Bauhaus, a design movement that sought to close the gap between art and industry. In 1941, Landor moved to San Francisco and established his firm, first known as Walter Landor & Associates (his wife served as his first associate). The firm began a movement to shape and edit carefully what became known as corporate identity—the way companies are seen. In 1964, Landor moved his office to a decommissioned ferryboat called the *Klamath*. The boat provided a great image for his firm, and on board employees worked in an easygoing atmosphere of creativity that belied the intense professionalism of the business. Landor Associates set the style for thousands of "creative" firms in later decades—small, personal, with global clients and freewheeling working practices.

Landor hung out with some of the most creative, edgy people of his time. A famous "gathering of communicators" aboard his boat in 1965 brought together writer Tom Wolfe, avant-garde thinker and communications theorist Marshall McLuhan, and West Coast adman Howard Gossage. The *Klamath* was described by Wolfe as a "great package design flagship." While aboard the docked ship, McLuhan, the author of the seminal book examining how information shapes consciousness, *Understanding Media,* predicted disaster for Landor's field. "Of course," he said in a characteristic McLuhanism reported by Wolfe, "packages will be obsolete in a few years. People will want tactile experiences, they'll want to feel the product they're getting. Goods will be sold in *bins*. People will go right to the bins and pick things up and *feel* them rather than just accepting a package." Landor, a physical package designer by trade, apparently just stood by and kept his cool.

In 1989, Landor, still chair of his own firm, which now had yearly revenues of around $50 million, sold its seventeen worldwide offices to ad giant Young & Rubicam. The firm had gone far from its days on the boat. These days, word on the street is that you will never get fired for hiring Landor. The aphorism speaks positively to Landor's long history of good work. But in a field that was once fueled by more revolution than evolution, it's also a backhanded compliment. In other words, hiring Landor is no longer a high-risk proposition, and sometimes getting the best creative work should involve risk. The firm helped name JetBlue Airways and Lucent Technologies and has a long client list that includes FedEx, KFC (the former Kentucky Fried Chicken), the Olympic Games, and Hyatt.

As it took on larger companies and its reputation developed and prospered, Landor worked increasingly with the most conservative corporations that clamored for vague, synthetic names. Landor has developed more than a few of these super-synthetics, most notoriously *Altria,* the new name of the Philip Morris Company.

Philip Morris was the consummate umbrella brand, but its parent company name was associated with one controversial product—tobacco. In November 2001, the company announced that it would assume a new name—Altria, which became a synthetic umbrella over Kraft Foods and the Miller Brewing Company (soon sold), as well as its several tobacco companies. In an advertisement, the company announced that Altria was "derived from the Latin *altus,* meaning 'high.' Altria symbolizes our company's desire to reach even higher . . . Our portfolio has diversified to the point that it now warrants a corporate identity that is equally broad-based." The reality was that this company constantly lived under the shadow of its tobacco dealings, and a name change could sever this connection in the public's mind. The name seemed a thinly veiled attempt to leverage the word "altruism."

More and more, companies like telecom giant Verizon (which was once a merged company consisting of the former Bell Atlantic, GTE, and Vodafone AirTouch) change their name to whatever they want—names that people then adopt. This new breed of synthetic names speaks of a new kind of company, one that can expand into a range of areas and industries without causing any major confusion in the marketplace. In 1853, Générale des Eaux started as a French drinking-water company, over time emerging as a conglomerate with wide-ranging interests in waste treatment, real estate, telecommunications, and media (among others). By 1998, the company, during a frenzy of acquisitions, renamed itself *Vivendi* (from the Latin verb *vivere,* to live) with a broad mission "to improve the standard of living for everyone." After merging with Seagram and its Universal Studios and Universal Music in 2000, the company became *Vivendi Universal,* a truly vague name that positioned the company as futuristic, not tied to any past or geographic locale. A lot of meaningless names—like *Verizon*—are created because of a trademark squeeze, and because corporations increasingly need larger umbrellas to fit all of their functions under.

As wide-ranging as the umbrella names may be, they are often shifted around. In August 2003, Vivendi Universal sold its entertainment assets to General Electric for $3.8 billion, which then renamed its NBC division *NBC Universal*. WorldCom changed its name in April 2003 to MCI, the name of its long-distance carrier, in a move to dissociate the firm from a major accounting scandal. Three and a half years after it merged to become AOL Time Warner, the largest media company in the world sought to distance itself from its troubled America Online division. As the grim business reality of the failed AOL Time Warner merger set in, what became surprisingly clear to anyone in the wordcraft business was that those three simple letters—*AOL*—were jeopardizing the future of the world's largest media company. In October 2003, the merged company lopped off *AOL* to become simply Time Warner—a draconian but essential step in reasserting the long-standing brand that had slowly expanded over the decades. Such an act suggests the power that even the components of the words—in this case just three letters that came to stand for the Internet itself—can have. The word *wordcraft* on the cover of this book borrows a *W* from the fast-food chain Wendy's—an old-fashioned-looking piece of type selected by a modern hamburger purveyor to suggest the flame-broiled Wild West; the more recent *O* from Orbitz, a manufactured font that, with circling arrows, embraces the idea of continuous, uninterrupted travel; the extended *R* from *Rolling Stone* magazine, which subtly conjures the rock 'n' roll injunction to "keep on truckin' "; the sans-serif *D* from Dunkin' Donuts, which announces itself through color more than style; the classic *C* from Campbell's Soup, an image that epitomizes a long-time American brand and calls Warhol to mind; a second *R*, this one from RCA, an acronym-turned-name with letters that once stood for the forgotten Radio Corporation of America; the *A* from ABC, another acronym but one that has a distinctly modern and unusual design; the Firestone *F*—another brand that made it through a life-threatening public relations crisis; and the *T* from Tums, a made-up word that is itself an abbreviation of the informal child's name—tummy—that this ubiquitous consumer product targets. In brand penetration, what one thinks of does not even have to be as big as a word; it could be a letter that, like these letters, works as a synecdoche to stand for the greater whole.

Although brands long have been associated with ownership, the essential role of the brand name and the brand image as we know it in the modern marketplace is a more recent phenomenon. Branding did not become a central concern to marketplace competitors until the twentieth century. Just one hundred years ago, food typically was bought from a shopkeeper who scooped brandless goods out of a barrel (an image that calls to mind Marshall McCluhan's statement about a future that has goods sold in bins). But as the idea of product selection entered the marketplace, one of the first tasks of branding was to bestow proper names on bulk foods such as sugar, flour, soap, and cereal—things that were once merely commodities. Originally the task of a shopkeeper was to label his flour as being from one or another mill; then that label itself could be leveraged not only to distinguish one purveyor from another but to advertise the qualities that become associated with the name of that purveyor in the marketplace.

In the late 1800s, corporate logos were introduced to mass-produced products like Campbell's Soup, H.J. Heinz pickles, and Quaker Oats cereal. Over time, names that acquired their own personalities or images—like Aunt Jemima and Old Grand-Dad—came to serve as ready-made advocates for products. "A nationwide vocabulary of brand names replaced the small local shopkeeper as the interface between consumer and product," write historians J. Abbot Miller and Ellen Lupton. This vocabulary has only expanded. And the recognized value of brand names also has grown; by the 1950s, companies came to realize that their brand identities were worth as much as the products themselves.

In the 1970s, a Chicago investment banker named Charles Shaw started a small winery in Napa, California. After a dozen years in the wine business he sold his winery—and his name—to a conglomerate called the Bronco Wine Company. By 2002, the wholesale price of bulk wine was so low that the conglomerate put together a new wine label, which it called Charles Shaw, and sold wine to consumers for less than two dollars per bottle. Bronco Wine sold its products under a number of labels, including Napa Ridge, a Napa-based winery that trucked in bulk wine from other parts of California. The Napa Valley Vintners Association even filed (and lost) a suit against Bronco, disputing its use of the name "Napa" for wine that was brought in from elsewhere. As for the Charles Shaw brand, the low price and decent taste earned the wine the nickname Two-Buck Chuck, and it sold so well that industry experts called it the fastest-growing table wine in U.S. history.

Brand names in modern commerce began by serving simply as labels to distinguish one product from others. And like all brand names through time, they were ways to ensure quality and reliability. Brands are forms of consumer protection—if there is a problem, the name gives a consumer a place to call. The oldest, those named for families or people behind products, known as eponyms, remain the most common form of brand names and use the integrity of a family name to ensure that one can associate a certain level of quality with a name (Smucker's, Levi Strauss & Co., etc.). Place names (American Motor Company) and descriptive names (International Business Machines) followed eponyms, later joined by made-up names like Kodak. We are now in the age of the umbrella name.

Umbrella names often have no inherent meaning; they are as far as one can get from the old notion of a brand as standing for one thing to differentiate it from another—like a type of flour from one or another mill. Almost all of the meaning in these umbrella names comes from the education that a firm provides. Landor had sent clients away with all-encompassing umbrella names so frequently that it had begun to draw industry criticism. The most pointed case of such criticism appeared in the online magazine *Salon* in Ruth Shalit's column. She posited that more and more companies were being given similar-sounding names—and not very good ones. Shalit pointed to Landor as a poster child of the new mediocrity, and she specifically referred to Landor's naming of Hewlett-Packard spin-off Agilent as a low-water mark. She quoted industry competitors who trashed the name: One said it was the "most namby-pamby, phonetically weak, light-in-its-shoes name in the entire history of naming" and called it a parody of a Landor name.

She was also not impressed by the naming of Bell Labs' spin-off, Lucent Technologies, another Landor fabrication. "In their zeal to professionalize and standardize what used to be a goofy, freewheeling, fly-by-night enterprise, the naming conglomerates tend to produce names that are reflective not of the client's corporate culture but of their own. The result: a slew of names that are sterile, antiseptic, talcum-powder bland," Shalit wrote.

Shalit's article did not go over well at Landor. Executives there had spoken frankly with her—but she made fun of them instead of parroting back everything they told her. Or rather, she made fun of them *by* parroting everything they told her. "This was similar to the Lucent process," David Redhill, global executive director at Landor, told Shalit about the name *Agilent*. "We needed a tremendous name that really was magisterial and compelling, and had a certain amount of stature right away." In their own words, it was clear that bureaucracy had come to envelop Landor, filling its talented troops with off-the-shelf thinking. The cult of personality that had been Walter Landor—once a real guy (like Arthur Andersen) who had real ideas about new things, ideas that could adjust and alter corporations—had departed. The soul had left the building. With its layers of deadwood, the firm that had descended from one of the creators of modern brand identity now could not even define its own identity and appeared to be suffering from a rarefied case of corporate groupthink.

Without trying too hard, Shalit had poked holes through the fabric of Landor. She didn't buy the Landor spin, because there was no spin. In my first contact with Landor, I got a sense that Shalit's column had wounded a few egos at the company, and I was told that it had created a defensive posture—something that I immediately picked up on. In the words of one guy at Landor, she basically painted naming as a racket—"Here's a name, now give us $40,000."

When I finally spoke with Landor's naming people, they didn't really dispel this notion. The truth is that it's hard to defend against this kind of criticism. No one at Landor would admit that sometimes all a naming firm really does is provide a well-lubricated process to generate a new name, presenting an objective framework that stands somewhat isolated from a corporate political bureaucracy. And it's clear from watching the Andersen videotapes that Landor was not driving the big thinking behind the project. The Landor people served as an outsourced provider of a process that managed thousands of name candidates and ran them through legal screening.

Anthony Shore, a creative director at Landor, leads what the firm has called its "verbal branding practice." This group creates brand lines—built to be somehow longer-lasting than mere slogans (one for Frito-Lay: "Food for the fun of it"). Shore led the Andersen Consulting naming process. Shore wears his wavy brown hair long, dresses like a graduate student headed to a job interview, and has a surfeit of nervous energy. Maybe he would set me straight about the awesome nature of umbrella names, the durability of synthetics over natural names. During our first meeting, I wanted very much to put Shalit's point of view aside and to listen to Shore hold forth about the vitality of his department.

Shore has a big role in the video sequences documented by Andersen. In one, he introduces what wound up as the winning name, saying that Landor linguists had determined that when spoken fast, the name sounds like *accent your*. But I did not learn much during my meeting with Anthony Shore that I did not already know. "We needed volume and exhaustive rigor," Shore said. "The namers we worked with were chosen for their thinking and their ability to work with language as basic matter. By having a wide variety of types of people contributing creative work, you ensure that the results will be equally diverse and fresh."

Despite this company line, Landor was not thrilled at first that Andersen Consulting was encouraging its employees to think up names. Nevertheless, it swung into action, developing list after list of names by following various strategies—including one in which only names beginning with "Ac-" were allowed, according to a former Landor creative. Landor generated some 3,000 names. Andersen Consulting employees turned in another 2,600.

A Numbers Game

As the pool of registered trademarks has expanded, so, too, has the difficulty in finding a suitable name for ventures, products, and services. Because there are so many different types of products and companies in the market, the United States Patent and Trademark Office (USPTO) sometimes allows one name to be registered as a trademark for two or more different companies, products, or services, so long as they are different enough that consumers will not be confused by the multiple uses of the name. The USPTO divides the market into forty-two classes, each composed of similar companies, products, or services. The same name may be registered as a trademark for more than one company, product, or service so long as the classes they belong to do not overlap. The trademark *Sonata,* for example, is a car manufactured by Hyundai Motor Company, a biological pesticide manufactured by Agra Quest, and a drug to treat insomnia, produced by Wyeth Consumer Healthcare. When you apply for a trademark, you designate which class or classes your trademark will fit into. There are thirty-four goods classes and eight service classes. A name can be protected in multiple trademark classes, assuming each one is relevant to the product or service's business area. Homophonic trademarks, which are spelled differently but sound the same, usually are not cleared for registration in the same class.

At its outset, the Andersen master list had almost six thousand names. This list was reduced twice; in the second round 440 remained, of which 161 were employee-suggested names. Of the 48 names from that round that met positioning and personality criteria and were selected for formal testing around the world, employees had submitted eight. More than twenty-five law firms in forty-nine countries conducted more than three thousand trademark searches to determine the availability of candidates. Some names thrown out early on had a similar tendency to use disfigured pieces of words: *Accelerated Commerce, Ciprocate, Empatic, Engenic, GoVantage, Nective, PlainSight, Revelist, Strataprise,*

Strateger, The Art of Change, Solutionary, WorldWise. Eventually, Landor whittled the list to around thirty candidates.

During a partners' meeting in October 2000, two months before deadline, Jim Murphy, Andersen's marketing head, unveiled the final pool of names, and the presentation was captured on film. Cued to music, Murphy ran a quick slide show. Each of thirty words flashed onscreen, set out in a different font: *About-Change, AcceleratedCertitude, AcceleratedChange, Accenture, ActiveChange, Adavis, AddCertainty, Ampatic, Archetypes of Change, Architects of Commerce, Architure, AvantGuide, Avizia, BrightEdge, Ceragence, Chasm, Encurve, Engence, Everise, Finesis, FutureSeek, Haliageny, Illinium, LightCurve, LightSeek, Lytro, Mentium, Menzana, Oriens, Refount.*

"You just saw our new name," says Murphy, pausing for effect. "The problem is we don't know which one it is yet." One can only imagine the feeling experienced by partners in the audience, forced to choose from such a list. They were left to ponder the implications: "I'm from *Menzana,* here to streamline your company. No. What about *Haliageny?*" As a group, the words were almost parodies—botched surgeries on words that mashed together parts of adjectives that had something to do with the aspirations of the people at the company. "This has been one of the most thorough name examinations that's ever been done by mankind," Murphy told the group with gravity that recalled a lunar landing.

When the 1,250 partners all voted on the names Murphy showed them, *Accenture* came out as a slight favorite. It was a flexible name, Anthony Shore told me—in large part because it was not descriptive of specific goods and services and, in his words, "captures the spirit of the organization." Because the market is constantly changing, the company would have to evolve to reflect the marketplace's needs and wants. To Shore, a name like *Accenture* would allow the company to withstand the test of time.

"*Accenture* arrived with the right amount of meaning," he said, "Such that it captures the spirit, but it does not limit them to what they can do."

The internal contest generated thousands of submissions from worldwide employees, who contributed words in fifteen languages: Arabic, Baule, Breton, English, Esperanto, French, German, Greek, Italian, Japanese, Latin, Sanskrit, Spanish, Swahili, and Thai. The winning word was born in the mind of one blond-haired, blue-eyed Dane named Kim Petersen, who worked in Norway. In a live company-wide meeting broadcast over the Internet in October 2000, managing partner Joe Forehand announced the chosen word to consultants all over the world. Petersen, who still did not know he had won the internal contest, was flown from Scandinavia to London the day of the announcement. The more formal public announcement followed in January.

As it happened, *Accenture* was the only finalist name that came from an employee. Sitting with Forehand and looking a little startled to be presenting to his worldwide colleagues for the first time live on the Internet, Petersen explained just how he came up with the name. "I thought it was a good suggestion," he began, "but I thought it would never have been chosen. There are so many bright people here. But I thought, 'It's worth a shot.'"

On September 14, 2000, Petersen had sat down at his desk in Oslo, Norway, to compose an email. The email was due the next day; there was little time to write. Petersen joined more than 2,600 of his colleagues at Andersen in a company-wide effort. Petersen's email focused on one word, *Accenture,* followed by a required fifty-word essay explaining why this word made sense as the new name for Andersen Consulting. "When trying to come up with a new name for the firm, I thought of things like bold growth, operational excellence, and a great place to work," says Petersen. Like most of the hard-working consultants who put in long hours for the worldwide firm, Petersen did not have a whole lot of time to dream up the absolutely ideal name. He jotted down his thoughts in the fifty-word micropitch, pointed to an "accent on the future," and zipped it over the wires to a centrally designated email address housed on a server at global headquarters in Chicago.

Before I talked to Petersen, Andersen's PR representative told me I would find a very nice, charismatic, articulate young man—in short, a perfect person to do interviews with people like me. Petersen, thirty-six, had been with the firm for the eight years since his formal education ended. He specialized in systems integration and worked in retailing with a focus on supply-chain issues. He said he had followed the arbitration process and had often discussed hypothetical names with his colleagues over lunch. "What are the core values of the firm?" he had wondered.

As he saw it, the company was trying to find one word that would encompass what it was—or wanted to be. Concepts that came to him included the notions of leadership, working with the best clients, and an outstanding work environment. He asked himself what the common denominators were. He took the word parts *acc-* from *accent* and *accomplish,* *-cent-* from the new century and the center of a network, and *-ure* from *future* and *adventure.* Later, he told me, the vision of the company, which he'd heard Forehand articulate, was *to create the future of its clients.* From that he extrapolated a sentence, "Accent on the future," and merged it into a name.

These days Petersen is used to seeing or hearing the word twenty times a day. "It's like your last name. It becomes part of you," he says. And indeed, after the firm poured more than $100 million into promoting the word through advertising all over the world, it grew to be much greater than just the three syllables stuck together by a single consultant in Oslo. The massive campaign foisted the word on businesspeople and potential clients all over the world—it would find them wherever they were. They would be *educated* about the new name, whether they liked it or not. They would be told that Accenture was a new way of doing business, that Accenture was a list of services, not just consulting, that the name was just one small part of what the company had changed.

It was a coup for the firm that an employee had coined the name. Petersen came to serve as the human-interest story behind the story, the soft-spoken and humble man who was thrust into the media spotlight. He took the vacation in Australia with his wife to observe an Accenture-sponsored golf tournament where an Accenture blimp hovered overhead. By the time he got back to Oslo, the signage on his office had been changed to read "Accenture."

Andersen Consulting attracted the interest of marketing writer Al Ries in 1997, who wrote presciently in his book *Focus*: "Andersen Consulting is a big success story, but the name is a potential anchor that will someday limit their growth. 'But we're too big and too successful to change our name' is the usual response of successful companies like Andersen Consulting. Actually, the bigger you are and the more famous you are, the easier it is to establish a new name. The media will do the job for you."

Jim Murphy, Andersen's head of marketing, conceded the point: "Al Ries is right," he acknowledged. "It's hard to change names." He also recognized the power of the media to spread the word. And Accenture was a good story: It involved a divorce and a $10 billion company losing its name, a dramatic proposition.

Andersen spread the word on its story. Publicity materials trumpeted that the Accenture "wordmark would be at the center of the largest and most pervasive business-to-business rebranding campaign ever conducted," which would include a global advertising investment of $175 million. The word itself, according to the company, embodied the firm's new marketplace positioning as a market maker, architect, and builder of the new economy and a "combination of 'accent' and 'future' that means to accelerate, to amplify, and to exceed expectations."

Accenture could have been renamed just about anything that could clear the remarkable number of hurdles in front of ownership. The name works in large part because of the financial resources behind it, the ability to fund its travel into the vocabulary of its target audience. It does not seem to come from a human voice; it sounds almost computer-generated, representative of a plastic culture.

In scripted remarks, managing partner Joe Forehand saluted the new name: "Accenture expresses what we have become as an organization, as well as what we hope to be—a network of businesses that transcends the boundaries of traditional consulting and brings innovations that dramatically improve the way the world works and lives." After Accenture was announced to the public in October 2000, Arthur Andersen stated that it was not happy with the name, that it was too close to Andersen Consulting (and indeed, with its first letters of *A* and *C* parallel to the old initials, and a similar number of letters, it did retain a connection). A lawsuit was threatened but never filed.

On the auspicious date of January 1, 2001 (or 01.01.01, as the advertising materials had it), Andersen Consulting became Accenture. Print and television ads flooded the marketplace. Urban financial districts and international airports were covered with Accenture propaganda. The London *Financial Times* was sponsored, for a day, by Accenture. Buildings were wrapped in signage reminiscent of the artist Christo's work. Young & Rubicam unleashed an extensive advertising campaign. One ad boldly declared: "In a bid to seize the future, Andersen Consulting redefines its field as Accenture. You might say our name was one of the smaller things we changed." Materials went out to clients all over the world introducing the new company, and showing how to pronounce the name (ak-*SEN*-chure). (In fact, it would be pronounced slightly differently in various parts of the world, which Anthony Shore defends by saying it gives people greater affinity to a name; they can pronounce it as their language's phonology allows them to.)

Before and after a brand is named, Landor conducts what it calls a verbal audit, poring over the wealth of written material that a company is using to determine how the imagery and message of the company comes across to outsiders. The verbal audit of Accenture conducted prior to the rebranding came out better than one in spring 2001. Some documents showed the word "Accenture" on the cover but mentioned "Andersen Consulting" throughout the document—showing what one former Landor staffer called a "schizophrenic" presentation. The verbal audit showed that Accenture was not communicating the idea it wanted to communicate. Yet, according to Poggenpohl, the name caught on fast and was quickly recognizable all over the world— a few minor mistakes in failing to change the name did not detract from the far-reaching global brand-name change.

According to Accenture's internal research, just before the name change, half of all senior executives in the United States were familiar with the name Andersen Consulting. Six months following the name-change announcement, there was a 70 percent retention of former awareness globally and 90 percent in the United States.

Dartmouth business professor Kevin Keller, the expert witness at the ICC trial, went on to write a case study about the transition. To Keller, the naming effort was noteworthy because of its massive scale, its speed, and the skill with which the name was implemented. He asked his students to think before class about the following questions: 1. What is different about branding a

professional services brand? What did Accenture do well in building the Andersen Consulting brand? 2. Was the choice of the
Accenture name appropriate? Evaluate the strategy and implementation behind the name change. 3. How should Accenture
arrive at a new positioning? How flexible or rigid should a positioning be? What recommendations would you make?

These were the questions Poggenpohl and her team had answered, they hoped, in full. *A professional services brand has to be
fluid and able to change with the times; Andersen Consulting had
grown over time to encompass effectively a wide range of services;
the name had been implemented well through vast ad campaigns;
the new positioning should lead the market and be flexible, not
rigid.* In his case study, titled "Accenture: Rebranding a Professional Services Brand," Keller laid out how Andersen Consulting
had pioneered the use of advertising as a way to build demand for
its services. To Keller, there were pronounced reasons why branding had come to the fore in corporate strategy since the late
1980s. "There was a realization that in competitive marketplaces,
brands matter. That is your enduring value. And you want to
brand yourself because you want to create differentiation. As the
market got more competitive, people realized that brand was this
weapon they had and they wanted to use it properly."

Cutting Loose

Of course, the name change turned out to be a blessing in dis-
guise. Former sibling Arthur Andersen was dragged onto center
stage in January 2002 with the well-exposed collapse of Enron
and Andersen accountants' role as paper shredders and document
destroyers. Having had a whole year to build up its brand, Accenture sailed free of the mess. Jim Murphy had stated in the
documentary video, "We need to eliminate all residual confusion

between ourselves and Arthur Andersen, no matter what they do with the Arthur Andersen name." Arthur Andersen, of course, ruined that once-good name through its involvement in Enron's downfall. And Enron was really just the next in line of high-profile fraudulent audits given the stamp of approval by Andersen, which started with Sunbeam and Waste Management and was followed by Global Crossing, Qwest, and WorldCom. For a firm that, from the very beginning, had built itself on impeccable judgment, falsifying audits was the ignominious end to the legend Arthur Andersen had launched in 1913.

Starting in March 2002, worldwide Arthur Andersen employees began defecting to competitors. In May 2002, the federal government brought the firm to trial under obstruction-of-justice indictments (after more than one deal with the government faltered), but by that point the firm's name already had been ruined and its partnership structure almost totally dismantled. A long list of Arthur Andersen clients, blue-chip companies such as Oracle and United Airlines' parent UAL, fired the firm after questioning its candor, as it admitted to having shredded documents that, presumably, would have linked it to Enron's demise. "The Andersen name is likely to live on in the popular culture as Watergate did, a shorthand way to refer to a certain kind of scandal," wrote *BusinessWeek*. "Andersen is now a very lame horse," former chair of the Federal Reserve Paul Volcker told the *New York Times*. "A lame horse that got shot in the head."

Some speculated that the combination of auditing and consulting within the same firm led to conflicted interests—and to the poor judgment the company showed with Enron. In the years leading up to the Enron debacle, the United States Securities and Exchange Commission had tried to pass auditor-independence rules to restrict the ways accounting firms both audited and consulted for the same clients. Arthur Andersen, a firm that offered both consulting and auditing, had long opposed such rules on the grounds that its auditing work was unimpeachable.

In the wake of the Arthur Andersen scandal, other consulting firms with strong links to auditing firms immediately began re-branding. PwC Consulting, the consulting division of Pricewater-houseCoopers, was the first to announce a new name—*Monday*. Although launched with great fanfare (full-page *Wall Street Journal* ads, etc.), the name was shelved when the company was bought for $3.5 billion by IBM—as PwC Consulting. Deloitte Consulting told me it wanted a "human" name for its newly split-off group, presumably in comparison to Accenture, and an-nounced, but never launched, *Braxton* (the name of a company previously acquired). "Let's face it, the world is tired of coined, invented, and whimsical corporate names," said chief marketing officer Brian Fugere. KPMG Consulting rechristened itself *Bear-ingPoint* to suggest the company's "commitment to set a clear direction" and to underscore its separation from KPMG's ac-counting functions. BearingPoint would go on to spend more than $30 million in changing its name.

It was an amazing, industry-wide case of groupthink. Names were supposed to offer a consumer a way to differentiate one en-tity from another—but suddenly, almost overnight, all the players had changed, leaving no constant. *Braxton! Monday! Bearing-Point! Accenture!* The consulting firms had, in lockstep, aban-doned their clubby law-firm names and taken on a batch of newfangled, synthetic, futuristic names. To help clients reach the future, they felt compelled to rename themselves accordingly.

Without ties to the past, Accenture was given free rein to in-vent its future—and therein lay the challenge. *Accenture* was a wholly new name—an empty vessel, a vessel waiting to be filled with new meanings. When people first heard the word, unvar-nished and standing alone, unsupported by any other messages, it meant little. It had no great message. It did not have one voice. Getting the message out, filling the vessel, would be the work of Poggenpohl's division. With time and even more money, *Accenture,* if properly played out, would come to represent the way for people to see what their own company did in a new light. It would cease to be about "speaking with one voice" and instead be about helping clients to take their own ideas and build on them.

The first advertising campaign following on the name-change announcements was one largely geared toward redefinition, putting *the idea* and its role in corporate achievement in the limelight. It was an interesting choice, a forward-thinking move to seize the high ground in a new alignment of business—one in which concepts tended to trump actual things.

At the start of 2003, Accenture pushed an all-new "I am your idea" advertising campaign: "I am your idea: Competitors may be closer than they appear." Ad copy read: "It's not how many ideas you have. It's how many you make happen. So whether it's your idea or Accenture's, we'll help you turn innovation into results." Accenture's own brand line was "Innovation delivered." "There is no shortage of ideas—be they yours, ours or anyone's," the ad copy went on. "But real, lasting competitive advantage only comes to those who fulfill and realize ideas." This was the campaign that would fill the vessel.

After a legal battle that could have destroyed the company, Andersen Consulting created a word that traveled large distances rapidly and was understood by the company's key target audiences—people inside the company, people whom the company was recruiting, and current and future clients. Because it had a window of time when the media was guaranteed to pay attention, the company just needed a word to let it tell its own story—a story not so much about *consulting* as about helping clients to move into the future in any and every way.

Accenture and BlackBerry would have different types of relationships with their customers. BlackBerry, just as Will Leben had described it to me, would be like its fruit counterpart. It would be something people would want to pick up. Accenture, on the other hand, would not want to be discovered in this way. There would be a lot of focus on telling people about the company—through advertising, in large part. The mission would not be to have people discover the company but to learn about a redefined company, one that had shed its strict management consulting roots and moved on. BlackBerry is something you want to pick up, Accenture is not. Both names achieved their objectives. BlackBerry was very much a bottom-up approach and Accenture a top-down approach.

An idea is "something one thinks, knows, or imagines." There seemed an inherent message in Accenture's new advertising that business was largely about ideas, that the companies with the best ideas would come out on top. Accenture seemed to be in agreement with what I was witnessing—that businesses were more and more idea-driven. And the funny thing was that Accenture's plan to help other companies turn their ideas into reality was not far from the idea of a brand name—which, if communicated well, would plant an idea in people's minds.

INTO THE
VERNACULAR

6

To get a fix on how ownership relates to language, it helps to look at an analysis of computer code, of which there are two basic types: open-source and closed-source. Code that is closed-source is controlled by its owner. Apple Computer owns the Macintosh Operating System—and its code is not available to non-Apple code writers. A code writer at Apple writes in this computer language, and when a program is complete, this code is transformed into binary code, a series of ones and zeros that can't be understood by others. Linux, on the other hand, is an open-source code, and any programmer can use it to write programs. Programmers also can help improve it. Software is developed by programmers who distribute the code without charge and then cooperatively debug, modify, and improve the software.

Open-source code turned the notion of code ownership on its head. Instead of one central code keeper—like Apple—code became a patchwork of different writers' work, a group effort of sorts, that could be constantly improved. Instead of a top-down code that one has to purchase, one can instead access for free the basic code building blocks and add one's own ideas and improvements. Launched in 1991, Linux has taken off; by 2002, 27 percent of all servers—corporate, academic, and retail—ran Linux.

To Lawrence Lessig, a Stanford Law School professor who specializes in issues related to the Internet, computer code is akin to language. In his 2001 book *The Future of Ideas,* Lessig equates language to open-source code—it resides in people's minds and they share it at will with no central owner interfering. In this way Linux can spread and improve faster than closed code.

Brand names and all trademarked words are more like closed code. A company that owns a trademark—like *Accenture, FedEx, Coca-Cola,* or *Levi's*—has a certain amount of control over how the word is used. Andersen Worldwide, after a legal battle, came to own Andersen Consulting's name but no other part of that company. These closed words cannot be used, for example, by a competitor or in many media without permission of the owner. Trademark law governs the way people traffic in trademarks—the closed code of the language. Unlike the English language, closed code has a definite owner, even though it is made up of pieces of "free" English language. Anywhere that closed code ends up, it's still owned.

One of the chief brand artifacts, as Hugh Dubberly would put it, is the verbiage associated with a new product or service. Traditionally the goal of any entity launching new words tied to its product or service has been to *own* these words, and trademark law provides the tools of ownership. On the face of it, ownership makes sense. If you spend any money advertising your particular word—Budweiser beer or Yoplait yogurt or Kibbles 'n Bits dog food—and get people to share some experience that they equate with your name, then you certainly don't want anyone else using your name. Or do you?

That Linux took off shows that ownership is not necessary for success. If you create something so intrinsically sound as Linux, it will move because of its quality. And it turns out words are not so different, that hardwiring a word with the right message from the beginning and letting it run free, like one of Maverick's cows, can be a compelling option. The question for anyone launching a word is how best to get the word *out there*.

Verbs in Play

Federal Express was started as a package delivery service by Fred Smith in 1971. By 1983, the company's annual revenues reached $1 billion. Many customers began to abbreviate the company's name to *FedEx* and even took to using the term as a verb—"I'll fedex the tickets to you." In 1994, the company formally adopted FedEx as its primary brand name.

Traditional thinking is that a company needs, at least conceptually, to own a word or, preferably, an idea. Jean-Marie Dru, a French advertising executive and author, writes of "the necessity of owning a word the way [FedEx] owns *overnight* . . . [as a verb]. . . . You have to own something. That's the only way for a vision to be effective and stand the test of time. You have to own an idea." Sometimes owning an idea is as easy as being the first one to talk about something—like FedEx talking about shipping overnight.

Gayle Christensen, director of global branding for FedEx, told me: "The use of FedEx as a verb is a double-edged sword. We cannot control the way the public uses our name in speech, but it's not something that *we* would do ourselves." In saying this, Christensen has to toe the legal line. But the reality is that for the owner of a name, it is ideal when consumers adopt a name into their own lexicon.

The intricate balancing act of trademark law hinges on the fine line that the trademark owner must draw between disseminating and protecting the word he owns. Trademark law often works to keep words *out* of common speech—to retain words as uppercase adjectives (Sheetrock Brand Gypsum Panels) and prevent them from becoming a lowercase noun or even a verb (to *sheetrock* the garage). But when a word slides into generic use, it gains power as an idea. The word enters the lexicon with its associations usually intact. "To sheetrock" means to put up gypsum wallboard. It also means to make a wall that's thin but rock-solid, the kind of stability sold in convenient sheet form. Indeed, the best names *are* ideas.

When I write that I *rollerbladed* down the street, *xeroxed* a couple of pages, *googled* someone, or *tivoed* a television show, I use brand names as verbs. "Verbed" brand names have transformed into ideas, tools that help people get by in a complex world. (Some companies have tried to prompt a wider cultural adoption of their products by using their own name in a verb form. Cuervo, the Mexican tequila brand, has run ads that take off on the Latin phrase *veni, vidi, vici*: "We came. We saw. We Cuervo'd.")

It's easier to say "Pass me the Coke" than "pass me a cup of carbonated syrup water," and it's much easier to say "Let me take a Viagra" than to get into specifics about why the pill is needed. The best words not only will fit in, they also will serve as tools. In *Acts of Meaning*, cultural psychologist and cognition expert Jerome Bruner cuts to the heart of this idea with a notion from computing. In "classic information theory," Bruner writes, "a message is informative if it reduces alternative choices."

Al Ries, the marketing author, points out the importance of individual words. "Most products are bought verbally, not visually. Even lettuce (Foxy), oranges (Sunkist), bananas (Chiquita), and other products are coming to the market with names attached.

The mind pays attention because the words add meaning to the products." Words, he says, "trigger meanings which are buried in the mind." Instead of just being a generic head of lettuce, a branded version—Foxy Lettuce—will trigger other ideas one has about foxes or foxy as an adjective for attractive. Sunkist similarly says "kissed by the sun," although most buyers do not consciously make this connection. "But what does it mean to own a position in the mind? Simply this: the brand name becomes a surrogate or substitute for the generic name."

The trick for anyone trying to get a message out is to understand *how* to trigger meanings. This is the ultimate task of the namer. New words launched into the language—and all words, really—exist by living in people's minds, by being a part of their vocabularies. New words that gain a substantial buy-in across many vocabularies and populate many textual sources, that wash up like flotsam on the beach of the ocean of language, are candidates to be dusted off and studied and possibly enshrined in the dictionary. These words have triggered meanings, and met with widespread adoption.

Into Dictionaries

Although one tends to think of a dictionary as an official repository of language, it is in reality nothing more than a snapshot of the language at one point in time. In his neo-dictionary *In a Word*, Jack Hitt solicited made-up words from people in a range of disciplines—words that did not exist but should. In the foreword to the book, Hitt paused to appraise the ungainly nature of traditional dictionaries: "Dictionaries are, when you think about them, unnatural. Language is a mess—massive spontaneous and deliberate combustions born out of the jabbering and scribbling of millions," he wrote. "English, especially as we Americans have remade it, is probably the most untamed and untameable language there is."

Anyone involved in name creation has to compete with this "jabbering and scribbling." And getting a word into the dictionary, especially the *Oxford English Dictionary,* is a form of validation. "It is often claimed that a 'word' is not a 'word' (or is not 'English') unless it is in 'the dictionary,' " reads the preface to the third edition of the *OED*. "This may be acceptable logic for the purposes of word games, but not outside those limits." When a new word enters the dictionary, that means it has gained widespread recognition. And it is notable when brand names enter the dictionary.

As snapshots, dictionaries allow us to gauge penetration—to gauge whether talk value has been achieved. And brands appear in the *OED* complete with definition, date of entry, and in-depth etymological data that provide a biography of each word. "Words, like individuals or nations, have complex and fascinating histories," write authors Sven Birkerts and Donald Hall.

Synthetic words have bloomed, populating the language like riotous spring flowers. After legal screening and international market research, these words are usually pleasing to the global ear. Trademarks are treated by the compilers of the *Oxford English Dictionary* just like other words that have made their way into the English language. A word generally is added to the *OED* when it is judged to be used by speakers without needing to be defined or attributed. The most recent print edition of the *OED,* the second, published in 1989, has 500,000 entries, of which about eight hundred are trademarks. Among the earliest trademarks to be included in the *OED* were Ichthyol (added in 1899) and Kodak (added in 1901). Four times a year the *OED* publishes new and revised entries to the *OED* on its Web site. In December 2001, it added *Dolcelatte, Halcion, Porta Potti,* and *Portaloo.* In March 2003: *Cineplex, Furby, Shake 'n Bake,* and *Beanie Baby.*

Alan Hughes, trademark editor for the *OED*, says that the *OED* decides to include a brand name when it has achieved a certain level of permeation of the English language. According to Hughes, "the main criterion for inclusion is the same as for other linguistic items, namely currency in published texts, whether newspapers, books, or learned journals." On this basis Hughes and his colleagues choose the words they wish to include in the *OED*, investigating the legal status of those they suspect to be trademarks. Words that are trademarks are noted as such in their entries. "In the case of trademarks in the *OED*, a word may cease to be a mark after publication of the entry, or conversely become one, in which case we would amend the entry accordingly." Sometimes, says Hughes, the *OED* is asked by a company owning a mark to remove the entry from the dictionary, a request they do not comply with. Once a word is in the *OED*, it has been validated by an expert team. The compilers of the *OED* do not recognize the legal standing of a word—just how far it has traveled, disseminated. To them all language is open-code.

Thinking about the dictionary allows one to see the language as a cohesive whole. In creating a new name, one has to create or find an existing word that will, essentially, fit well into the vocabulary of a customer. Unlike natural language, a product or company's name derives much of its meaning from the perceiver's experience of the names of similar things. But if there is little in the perceiver's experience that resonates with this name, there will be little recognition. In September 2001, two drug names entered the *OED*—*Prozac* and *Viagra*. Pharmaceutical namer David Wood had a leading role in the creation of both names.

LOVE IS
THE DRUG

7

In an inversion of the role of the professional namer, a novelist can drop a single trademarked word to sketch an entire world of meaning. In *A Supposedly Fun Thing I'll Never Do Again,* novelist and essayist David Foster Wallace writes that writers use brand names, what he calls "pop references," both to be realistic and to comment on the "vapidity of U.S. culture." Wallace notes: "Put simply, the pop reference works so well in contemporary fiction because (1) we all recognize such a reference, and (2) we're all a little uneasy about how we all recognize such a reference." This enables a writer to leverage a brand name to great effect because describing a character's relationship to a branded item (say a kid who hates *Nintendo,* an executive who wears *Armani*) often says more about that character than would any long string of adjectives.

Wallace describes a writing teacher he had who discouraged any use of brand names in literature and advised students not to use them because it would date their work. The students protested, arguing that because brand names were so ubiquitous in modern life, they would time-stamp a story no more than would the presence of a car. And not only do we all recognize the occasional brand name we read in a novel or short story but it often forces us to analyze the world we live in in a new way, opening our eyes to brand-name universality. Wallace himself references the omnipresent sponsorship, the effects of top-down naming efforts. Some of Wallace's novel *Infinite Jest* takes place in a world where even calendar years are sponsored, alternatively by the *Depend Adult Undergarment* and the *Trial Size Dove Bar*.

Novelists tend to foresee future speech saturated with trademarks. Writer William Gibson (coiner of the word *cyberspace*) envisions a black-market trade in brand-name eyeballs and brain implants, negotiations peppered with capitalized words. In *Pattern Recognition* his protagonist, whose job as a "coolhunter" is to spot new trends and advise advertising agencies and marketers how best to commodify them, is herself allergic to certain universal brands—Tommy Hilfiger and the Michelin Man in particular.

In Jonathan Franzen's National Book Award–winning novel, *The Corrections,* a college student swallows Advils and is seen "galloping across the Lucent Technologies Lawn" on a campus with a "Viacom Arboretum." Two fictional pharmaceutical companies loom in the background. One, Axon, is in trials for a drug named, unambiguously, Corecktall—a cure-all that will, like any futuristic pill, correct all ills. Drug names often appear in fiction, placed there by writers who seem to want to pause and consider the futuristic leaps that these products represent. Another Franzen-coined drug company, Farmacopea, makes a compound called Aslan (taken from the lion in C. S. Lewis's Narnia books). Through this last reference and one to the Toyota Cressida (a Shakespeare allusion), Franzen shows the way fiction and fact intertwine in the naming of things.

What does it mean, many seem to ask, that we all use corporate shorthand to describe ourselves and our feelings? What are the human implications that our thoughts turn to words like *Advil* and *Toyota* instead of generic terms like *pain reliever* and *truck*? The better writers incorporating brand names in fiction are fascinated and concerned about the implications of a language taken hostage by alien, capitalist-controlled, and commercially subservient words.

Indeed there is a constant back and forth between fact and fiction with brand names. And Walter Kirn noticed this when he wrote in *Up in the Air,* a novel about a frequent-flier traveling salesman: "Ambien. Dexedrine. Lorazepam. Names that are all connotation and assonance, Z's and X's for ups, and M's for downs. Is that where the poets have gone? To Merck and Pfizer?"

Is that where the poets have gone? That's what I wanted to know when I set out to meet the group of namers who have, in fact, given the world a majority of the drug names that fill millions of medicine cabinets. They don't work at Pfizer or Merck but at a consulting firm called Wood Worldwide. And the names they create become instant ideas.

The Ultimate Global Shorthand

David Wood, founder of Wood Worldwide, remembers the real beginning of brand awareness in the pharmaceutical industry. In 1979 Wood ran the U.S. office of Interbrand, which was then a startup branding firm. It now has grown into a worldwide franchise of one thousand employees and is owned by Omnicom, the world's third-largest advertising conglomerate. After a six-year stint at Interbrand, Wood left to found David Wood and Associates (later Wood Worldwide) and to focus exclusively on pharmaceutical clients. "We are up to our gunnels in drugs!" says Wood with characteristic enthusiasm. His first client, in 1987, was pesticide and herbicide manufacturer American Cyanamid.

Since the pharmaceutical industry experienced an exponential growth cycle in profits in the early 1980s, over-the-counter and prescription drugs have become popular-culture signifiers. Take *Prozac,* an invented word. David Wood, who helped coin the word in 1984, says, "It's short and aggressive; the 'Pro' is positive, and the z indicates efficacy." Zantac, an ulcer medication introduced in the 1980s, was the prototype for coined names. "The name was universally hated when it first came out," says Wood. But it went on to become a top-selling drug. Drug names used to sound a lot more like the scientific names that medical professionals used to describe them, names like *Ansaid, Adenocard,* and *Hydrodiuril.*

The name *Zantac* may have been so hated because it represented a shift from the scientific to the sci-fi. Drug names have progressed through three stages, from a first stage in which the medical and scientific components affected the name (*Lomotil*), into a second stage when they aggressively sought to stake out the future (*Xanax*), and into the latest stage of trying to be futuristic while rooted in the present (*Claritin*). The new names are somewhat more organic-sounding, as if the namers have lately realized that people would rather ingest things that sound pleasing— *Allegra, Propecia, Sarafem*—over things that sound space-age— *Zantac, Zocor, Zyrtec.*

Like *Paxil* and *Zocor,* many of the brand names invented by Wood Worldwide are now so-called megabrands. (In 2001, the firm was sold to rival Interbrand and renamed InterbrandWood Healthcare. For brevity's sake, it will be referred to here simply as Wood Worldwide. This group would get shuffled into the larger conglomerate, but I was interested in the group as I first found it—with its solid track record naming blockbuster drugs.) The work at Wood Worldwide spans a range of medical conditions, and includes the following: *Fuzeon,* for treatment-resistant HIV patients, for Roche/Trimeris; *Mevacor* and *Zocor,* cholesterol reducers for Merck; *Xubix,* a platelet-aggregation inhibitor for Roche; *Paxil,* an antidepressant for SmithKline Beecham; *Sonata,* a hypnotic compound for Wyeth; *Prilosec,* an anti-ulcer drug for Merck; *Pegasys,* a hepatitis C treatment for Roche; *Proscar,* an alpha inhibitor for Merck; *Teventa,* an incontinence treatment for Pfizer; *Valtrex,* an anti-herpetic for GlaxoSmithKline. As a group, these names tend to hide their definitions. Not so easily parsed, they give off generic good vibes: *Pegasys* conveys a fast-moving, airy feeling; *Paxil* offers a newfound peace; *Sonata,* a pleasant chorus.

Wood Worldwide has scored more than a few successes. Of the top ten best-selling drugs of 2002, the company named six: *Zocor, Prilosec, Eprex, Celebrex, Prevacid,* and *Paxil.* These words span the globe, filling television commercials and magazine advertisements . . . *Ask your doctor about Prilosec today.* The cost of consultation depends on the number of names evaluated, and industry costs range from $100,000 to $700,000.

David Wood himself has a friendly demeanor and a physician's knowledge of human physiology. He has thinning white hair and a white beard that traces his jawline and makes him appear more the salty fisherman than the senior executive of a brand strategy firm. When Wood speaks about pharmaceutical branding, he shows a love for what he does and a refreshing sense that his powerful, extremely wealthy corporate clients do not have a lock on his mind. To his colleagues he has a studied relaxedness, a mellowness that is almost shocking. He's someone you expect to lecture about gene mapping or osmosis, not his ideas for a Pfizer-sponsored Viagra clothing line.

It's fair to say that David Wood's theories concerning the marketing and selling of drugs skew a bit off-center, more in line, perhaps, with a world prophesied by fiction writers than reality. Wood says that drug companies like Prozac's Eli Lilly "think they are in the business of selling drugs to deal with depression, but they should think of themselves as making you feel terrific about yourself." He points out that Caterpillar, maker of the giant yellow earthmovers ubiquitous at construction sites, has played off its tough and dependable image in selling an exceptionally popular line of heavy-duty work boots. Eli Lilly could do the same with Prozac, Wood says, by merchandising the product in some creative ways that leverage its profound brand equity. After an interview with David Wood, I mistakenly wrote down that Pfizer had sponsored a Valentine's Day parade in New York City—a Wood idea, but not a reality. When I checked with Pfizer, my contact wrote back, "Viagra never sponsored a parade of any kind." For a moment I experienced the humorless world Wood and company face every day as they slowly alter it.

But regardless of whether they take all his ideas, Pfizer, Wood says, is an outfit that knows how to market. "We tell them not to sell drugs but perceptions," says Wood. "People should be fans of brands, like sports. We are trying to create a fan experience."

Early on, Wood Worldwide recognized that pills represented abstract ideas, and they incorporated that realization into their output. Patients, they determined, need tools to relate to the potentially embarrassing or hard-to-discuss situations they find themselves in—whether these involve impotence, depression, baldness, obesity, incontinence, or any of a wealth of predicaments that fill out the process of living. A strong brand allows patients to talk about their health issues at a distance; they can say "Prozac" rather than "depression," and uttering that word makes it less personal, less *their* problem than a universal one. It puts them in the world with others, not alone in the doctor's office. Pills, or more specifically the names of pills, are tools. If patients can talk about something, they will be a lot more likely to ask their doctors about a new treatment. For Merck or Schering-Plough, every time a patient remains quiet around a doctor, instead of asking for *Propecia* to treat baldness or *Claritin* to treat an allergy, a sales opportunity has been lost. These names have a sort of "advanced talk value," because when a patient discusses a condition by using its trademarked name, he literally increases the value of the medication to its owner.

"To be a big-time brand, you can't be one of the guys—you have to stick out like a sore thumb," says David Wood. "If a brand is a story, the brand name is its title. It may describe, it may suggest, it may evoke—and it may even provoke—but it always identifies the product and reinforces its uniqueness. The brand name is the hook that calls attention to the product." This hook is what his firm crafts. "Brands transcend language—they are their own language, that's the genius of brands," says Wood. "They are the ultimate global shorthand. We invent new language, and that is pretty awesome if you think about it. We are putting in place pieces of universal language, with no translation needed."

In the Wood method of pharmaceutical branding, altering the nomenclature that surrounds a drug is an essential part of the naming process. Rephrasing a condition using new language changes the way people perceive a disease and allows marketers to build or manufacture awareness of a so-called disease state. The drug firm Pharmacia rephrased urinary incontinence as *overactive bladder* for a drug called *Detrol*. Premenstrual syndrome became *premenstrual dysphoric disorder* (PMDD) for Eli Lilly's *Sarafem* (itself a rebranded version of Prozac). Bristol-Myers Squibb recast female facial hirsutism as *unwanted facial hair* (or UFH) for the drug *Vaniqa*. These are euphemisms, so obvious that they are funny. But they work. The way a pharmaceutical drug describes what it treats can be just as powerful as its brand name. And this added nomenclature helps to build the name into an idea that, in the minds of patients, becomes a tool to help them with a health problem. More than others, these names have to be targeted and specific, not at all vague. A word that surrounds a more typical product, like beer, is not so precisely aimed. It might draw out general associations connected with socializing and relaxing, but a pill has to point with laser precision. If the pill treats allergies, the consumer has to go through an almost robotic mind response: *I am experiencing a seasonal allergy, I need to consume one Allegra tablet right now.* And it's a sale that must happen not only once but again and again.

Marker Sniffing

In the early months, when my partner, Glasgow, and I were starting Quiddity, our naming firm, we got a call from Glaxo Wellcome, the international drug conglomerate that, following a merger in 2000, would become GlaxoSmithKline. The call came from a researcher named Jack, who had read the naming article I published in *Wired*. We were invited to visit the corporate headquarters in North Carolina and present for two hours—telling the assembled group about ourselves and also examining some possible names for a pill that was in the Glaxo pipeline. We had dipped our toes in healthcare, having just worked on a renaming project for a beleaguered hospital chain called Columbia/HCA that had overcharged Medicare and Medicaid, had stolen millions from the government, and was evaluating ways to distance itself from a sordid past. (We created dozens of names—the company ended up as simply *HCA*.)

For Glaxo, we had just a week to prepare for our presentation, and we spent it reading through a small library of medical texts. The task of naming a drug impressed both of us: the abstractness of putting a name to such an intangible product was challenge enough, but the huge reach that a major pharmaceutical drug would have—and the sheer amount of money involved—was awe-inspiring.

Because of strict confidentiality rules on the client's end, we were not quite sure what kind of pill we would be naming until three days before the pitch meeting. Our minds wandered through the possibilities. When we were not studying the larger trends that influenced the pharmaceutical industry, we talked loosely about the increasing role that pills played in society and the prevalence of self-medication. Glasgow commented that lots of people were taking mood-altering and mind-shifting medications simply to cope with the world around them. We wondered if we would be naming one of these new "lifestyle" drugs. It turned out Glaxo wanted us to help name a compound to treat HIV.

We crammed during those last three days, learning everything we possibly could about HIV and the drugs used to treat it. My brother, a resident in internal medicine, consulted with us over take-out Chinese in his on-call room. We logged on to chat rooms where HIV-positive patients communicated with doctors about incredibly detailed particulars related to specific drugs. Before leaving for North Carolina, we prepared a ten-page document that summarized our findings in what was, for us, technical language.

We arrived at the sprawling campus early enough to have time to browse through the display cases in the lobby that showcased Glaxo's many blockbuster drug brands. We noted that Glaxo's Zyban and Wellbutrin were the same drug, just marketed under different names as a means to combat smoking and ease depression, respectively. This phenomenon (as seen with Eli Lilly's Prozac/Sarafem) speaks to the power of a name, that a particular name targets the specific use and customer base of a product. We also laughed about the allergy drug name *Flonase,* which just did not seem like the best possible name, conjuring as it does the idea of flowing nasal cavities. (But maybe this direct contradiction is what somehow attracts.) Our host, Jack, met us and took us to a small auditorium.

Glasgow and I handed out our meticulously bound folders to a room of marketers, and we took the group through a description of naming conventions and then into some naming exercises. In one of these, we examined hypothetical ad campaign tag lines for product launches featuring this new HIV drug. In another exercise the group moved around applicable word parts to create new names. In the space of two hours we came up with some strong name possibilities for the new compound.

I don't remember exactly when Glasgow distractedly began to take whiffs of the pungent dry-erase marking pens that he was writing with, but by the time I noticed I was consumed by an uneasy feeling that our audience was not amused by our presentation. The audience, in fact, shrank from fourteen to four over the two hours we were there. As he walked us to the door, our host said something about "next time you all are here," and for me that was at least a glimmer of hope that we would be called back.

The truth was that when we flew to North Carolina we had no idea what we were getting into. Most naming projects face enough obstacles in securing a trademark and a domain name. But all the creative ideas out there do you no good when naming a pharmaceutical drug. You have to clear dozens of trademark and regulatory roadblocks. It wasn't until I met David Wood that I really understood why we never had a chance with Glaxo. We had only a general understanding of the notion of altering the nomenclature of diseases. And drug names, more than any other named things in the world, must answer to many masters. We had little chance of success in delivering a name to Glaxo because we lacked the support team necessary to clear the formidable hurdles drug names face, and we lacked a well-crafted sales pitch to sell ourselves to an industry wary of outsiders.

Side Effects

The amount of research, money, creativity, legal and scientific screening, and long-range planning that goes into each and every pharmaceutical brand name is immense. And as I got to know David Wood and his creative director, R. John Fidelino, I became more and more clear on just what it takes to launch a successful new drug name. The team at Wood Worldwide is quick to point out that the creative part of its work is only a fraction of the overall work done in shepherding names over steep regulatory obstacles. At Wood they've created what they call a ten-by-ten gauntlet, a filter through which they feed name candidates to test them against regulatory issues as well as lexical similarity to and confusion with other drug names. According to their research division, some 35 percent of the nine hundred drug names filed each month at the USPTO are rejected. But restrictions placed on drug names by regulatory bodies are just part of the equation. The advent of direct-to-consumer marketing and patent hurdles faced by these compounds, and the approval of generic forms of drugs, also have pronounced effects on drugs' names. The marketing of drugs changed profoundly in 1997 when the FDA amended its rules to let, for the first time, pharmaceutical companies advertise prescription drugs directly to consumers (albeit with certain restrictions).

Another special burden the pharmaceutical companies carry is that any slowdown in the naming process or clinical trials can cost millions of dollars in lost sales. The cost of developing a typical new drug is estimated to be $500 million, and the goal of each drugmaker is that, once in the market, the drug can more than recoup this stiff initial outlay. As soon as a drug patent is filed, a drug company has seventeen years to sell it exclusively. The longer it takes from the date a drug patent is issued to the date a new drug is released for sale, the fewer years of sole ownership during which the manufacturer can maximize the return on its investment. The time preceding Food and Drug Administration approval represents lost income to the firm—and a drug *must* have a name before the FDA will approve it.

One of the fascinating things about drugs, for a namer, is that they actually have several names. They are first given a chemical name, then a generic name, and finally a brand name. A chemical name is given when a new chemical entity (NCE) is developed. The chemical name specifies the molecular structure of the drug and is used primarily by researchers. The chemical name for Paxil, for example, is (-) -(3S,4R)-4-[(p-fluorophenyl)-3-[(3,4-methylenedioxy) phenoxy]methyl]piperidine hydrochloride hemihydrate. A generic name is typically created when a drug is ready to be marketed. Although the manufacturer of the drug has the exclusive right of manufacture during the years of the drug's patent, it never can own the generic name. Paxil is known generically as paroxetine hydrochloride. Prefixes, such as *pfi* for Pfizer or *gla* for Glaxo, which suggest a manufacturer's name, are not allowed; the generic name is a part of the public domain. Generic names are systematically created using stems, words common to members of a related group of drugs (a stem that unites sleeping pills is, for example, *olam;* alprazolam, midazolam, and triazolam are three). Federal law mandates the use of generic names in advertising and on labels and brochures.

The company that patents a drug creates the brand name. The FDA must authorize all drug labeling and approve all drug brand names. It is the governing body most responsible for whether a drug name gets approved. The FDA forbids use of words that make overt promises—such as "cure" and "safe." An antidepressant called *Panacea,* for example, would not meet with approval. The FDA rejects a third of all names submitted based on implied claims and conflicting and confusing names—*Rogaine* was originally called *Regaine* (implying, more directly, that hair would come back). The name may not encode or imply dosage, efficacy, or suggest off-label uses. It's interesting, though, what slight differences allow a name to pass muster. A slightly poetic twist in coining a word can garner FDA approval. A drug named *Halcion,* a sleeping pill that takes its name from *halcyon* (meaning peaceful), succeeds with just a slight spelling change that most consumers do not see as an overt brand message. You can't make an outright promise, but if your name conjures some poetic mythology, it might just be allowed. A sleeping pill named *Peace?* No. *Halcion?* Yes.

The most critical issue in drug name selection is the elimination of confusion among other drug names. A name must neither sound like that of another drug (which can lead to errors when verbal prescriptions are made) nor look like another drug name when written out by hand. The puzzle is in finding a name that is intriguing and appropriate, safe, distinct, honest, and not already trademarked. Wood once named an alcoholism treatment medication *Revia,* and then, after finding pronunciation difficulty in Hispanic populations (where the word sounded like the Spanish word for rabies), reformatted the word to ReVia.

The FDA tries to prevent trademark confusion by convening a committee of experts before each drug is approved. Reviewers check for conflicts with other products and for confusing names. Merck's ulcer medication was called *Losec* until post-launch mix-ups with *Lasix,* a diuretic, caused a patient's death. With Wood Worldwide's help, *Losec* became *Prilosec* (now the best-selling drug in the world). Celebrex, a best-selling arthritis and painkiller drug that was the first of a class known as Cox-2 inhibitors, was originally named *Celebra*. An internal competition at Monsanto's drug subsidiary G.D. Searle & Co. came up with that name, but in the end it did not meet FDA approval because it was so close to the antidepressant Celexa.

Drug companies now patent the process of manufacturing the raw drug compound, and they also can patent the trade dress—the size, color, and shape of the pill. These are all steps that allow drug companies to maintain market dominance longer and own market share in advance of generic drugs. Generic drugmakers, for their part, increasingly litigate against pharmaceutical companies as they seek to win the rights to make generic, less expensive versions of brand-name drugs.

Barr Labs is the most aggressive group in pursuit of the legal permission to produce generic forms of trademarked, patented drugs. Led by CEO Bruce Downey, Barr files suit against drug makers to contest their patents. In the face of such a challenge, drug companies often seek to extend patents by, among other things, applying to test the drugs for children and extending the use of the drug to other conditions. In 2001, Barr won a five-year fight with Eli Lilly to invalidate a critical patent on the $2.6 billion blockbuster antidepressant Prozac. The ruling gave Barr the right to sell a generic version of Prozac—fluoxetine—six months ahead of its competition. A year later, Barr was predicted to have sold $250 million worth of the unbranded drug—money that Eli Lilly could have earned had it won in court. Generic companies fill about 42 percent of all drug prescriptions in the United States, which accounted for around $20 billion in drug sales in 1999, while more expensive branded drug sales accounted for $90 billion.

Although the United States and most countries maintain intellectual property laws to protect patents and trademarks, laws do not govern patents in the same manner in India and a few other countries. More than a few large Indian companies reverse-engineer drugs manufactured in the United States and give them new names with clear links to their progenitors. In this way a form of Prozac was dubbed *Nuzac* and Viagra became *Erecto*. These companies, like Bombay-based Cipla Ltd., sell drugs for a fraction of what they are sold for in the United States. Yusuf Hamied, Cipla's managing director, has been called a pirate king by U.S. companies that maintain a vested interest in seeing that drugs or, to be more precise, their intellectual property, are not "stolen."

The back-end complications that drug names face demand a well-oiled machine, and Wood has a serious back end that can run the many checks to ensure a name's viability. On the front end, playing a perhaps smaller but more colorful part, stands R. John Fidelino.

Future Perfect

Fidelino spends a lot of his waking hours thinking about the future. In a state of constant fast-forward, he thinks about what the world will be like in five to ten years, and about how pharmaceutical drugs will help patients approach a range of issues. "To a certain degree, today is irrelevant," Fidelino tells me. "Today is a setup for tomorrow." Because language, and the language surrounding drugs, always develops, alters, and changes, Fidelino has to create words that will sound futuristic when they launch years after he has created them. Will a word like *Fuzeon* be dated by 2005? He has to know.

Because the marketing of drugs takes so much more preparation, testing, and analysis than the marketing of most other products, the namers have to build in a lag time and ensure that the name, when launched in two or seven years, will fit into an evolved lexicon. It's more challenging than, say, a computer network that will be named and launched within a year's time.

All products in development depend on predicting what the future will hold, but Fidelino's projects are further out than most. When Fidelino meets with his clients, typically the largest pharmaceutical companies (Pfizer, Merck, Roche, Novartis, etc.), he often is consulted regarding compounds or mere molecules—or even white-paper sketches of molecules. And when he's briefed on forthcoming drugs, the key expectations for the drug may not be confirmed, as scientists and researchers often don't want to commit to something that can't be proven. As creative director at Wood Worldwide, Fidelino creates names and, increasingly, nomenclature for clients whose products often take a decade from concept stage to marketplace. In that decade, cancer might be cured, AIDS eliminated, hay fever banished, malaria overcome, cloning made common, and life-prolonging drugs may become obtainable. It is up to Fidelino to suspend his disbelief and come up with the words that will sound just right for these treatments in the years ahead.

Going to great lengths to channel creativity, Fidelino comes up with new names by tapping enough representative minds to paint a broad picture, as well as by running lengthy brainstorming sessions and conducting assiduous exploration of technical details. Beyond his inside team, Fidelino at times turns to an outside pool of talent that includes the usual namers: poets, journalists, copywriters, dancers, artists, shoppers, and basically anyone who he feels has a "different mind and their own way of looking at the world."

Fidelino looks at trends and thinks through their relevance outside of him. It's about understanding the *beat,* he says, by which he means the vibe—the view of the industry in the future, from both an internal and an external view. "My role at the company," says Fidelino, "is to be constantly looking for trends, to understand what's next. I'm not a futurist, and I'm not an avant-gardist, either. I just want to know what's next." He can't create the words of the future unless he has a pretty good sense of what the future will hold.

"Advertising tends to focus on a particular moment in time, whereas branding is concerned with the entire lifecycle of the product—the entire time that the product is going to be out on the market, this brand has to exist," Fidelino tells me. "So you have to be able to forecast what its potential can be at every stage of its lifecycle, and create something that can stand that test of time."

In Fidelino's five years of service to the firm, he has built his own creative department. The group is far more ethnically diverse than you typically find in advertising—starting with Fidelino himself, who is Filipino-American. With their median age of twenty-seven, I came to think of them as "the kids" (although their ages would not stick out at all in a typical advertising agency or an Internet startup). It's both surprising and refreshing to find a group as young as this dealing with a typically stodgy industry. Their view of the pharmaceutical world is not yet jaded, and they have a closer connection to youth culture and its slang nuances. By the time many drugs make it out of trials and gain approval and find their way into doctors' hands, Fidelino's team will be the age of the target market. When you are living in the future, you have to build your team accordingly.

Fidelino is twenty-eight in a pharmaceutical industry heavy on middle-aged management. He readily admits that in his dealings with pharmaceutical executives he plays the youth card. If David Wood is the chief strategist, Fidelino is his youthful and turbo-charged deputy—creative in his own right and also capable of carrying out the larger mission of astonishing clients. The first time we met, he was wearing a tight, long-sleeved shirt with no collar, which left his midriff exposed when he tilted back in his chair, a look that was at first disconcerting because I expected to meet someone who exhibited the typical stuffiness I had seen at Glaxo years before. Fidelino looks more like he's headed out for an evening at a club—with fashionable clothing designed by Marc Jacobs and an up-to-the-minute haircut—than working in an office. His clothing choices suggest that he might have pondered what people might wear in the future, then gone and bought it. I soon realized it's a way to disarm clients—to show them that they have stepped into his world. And he's got the boundless energy to juggle more than three dozen drug-naming projects at any given time. Each project takes eighteen to thirty-six months.

Fidelino has much in common with those modern novelists and short-story writers who turn to brand names as a way to comment on the present-day culture and the future it will become. But Fidelino is no dreamy poet and comes to the job with a résumé fine-tuned for what he does.

Fidelino, like me and my business partner as well as a surprising number of others I have met in the naming industry, went to Brown University. In the early 1990s, courses in Brown's Modern Culture and Media (or MCM) department were exceptionally fashionable. They blended the study of literature, semiotics, and popular culture. In his book *One Market Under God,* business culture and advertising critic Thomas Frank questions whether the department was in place to train people to critique "the system" or to produce advertising, branding, and entertainment within it—presumably after properly deconstructing it. Cultural studies, like those found in the MCM department, writes Frank, were "becoming a more or less direct path into employment in the lucrative and fashionable business of TV, film and advertising production." It's a point that's hard to argue with; as one friend jokingly put it, "We were trained for good and put it to evil."

In this postmodern hothouse, Fidelino took a full load of pre-med courses. A lot of students at Brown take an introductory neuroscience course nicknamed simply "The Brain." Fidelino took the course and became interested enough to make neuroscience his major. One particular class, on aphasia—the total or partial loss of the power to use or understand words—influenced his thinking the most. "It opened my eyes to the relationship between speaking and understanding," he says, and it gave him ideas for later applications toward making language relevant. Fidelino's pre-med and science background helps him effectively identify the consumer base for particular drugs and lay out the qualitative objectives for a name.

To be sure, very little is concrete in Fidelino's world—his work starts with intangibles and ends with intangibles. Drugs are some of the most intangible goods in the marketplace (right next to perfume) and carry little, if any, packaging. It's like naming air—it's almost that vaporous. In the name, says Fidelino, "You try to talk about what it's for, but you might not be hitting the mark. We can't really talk about the pill shape. We can't necessarily talk about the molecule; it's not very interesting. We're interested in blazing a perception despite nothing tangible." When you add to the high intangible ratio in Fidelino's world another recent trend, the tendency of more pharmaceutical companies to address lifestyle questions, things get even less concrete.

Lifestyle Issues

The term "lifestyle drug" comes up frequently in the literature around modern pharmaceuticals, but it is dismissed around the Wood Worldwide offices. The term *lifestyle,* Fidelino told me, fails to acknowledge the gravity of life. "We don't even use the term *lifestyle,*" he says. "We just talk about hopes and the quality of life."

To pharmaceutical companies, lifestyle problems offer an opportunity to provide low-risk, long-term solutions with high returns on investment. The messages they promote are more positive and less life-threatening. A handbook on branding pharmaceutical drugs says it most directly: "This type of application offers manufacturers a more powerful platform for consumer brand building than the more scientific or medical one."

Traditional medical applications are concerned with treating, controlling, or reducing the risk of serious medical conditions like high cholesterol, heart disease, and diabetes. Lifestyle drugs treat physical presentation (like dental care, acne, aging, hair loss, and weight control), performance (mental concentration in the workplace, stress reduction, sexual performance), and general well-being (pain reduction, mood regulation, incontinence). Lifestyle drugs can make people's lives feel happier and more content (though not necessarily by curing a serious medical condition). Based on what they treat, lifestyle drugs have necessarily led naming trends in a more conceptual direction.

As the number of drugs that relate to lifestyle enhancement has grown, the patient-doctor relationship has shifted, too. Patients have started to see health care through the more aspirational messages of living better. Drug messages have evolved from addressing concrete problems to addressing lifestyle considerations—and doctors have followed that evolution as well. "Doctors might now say, 'How do you want to live your life? Explain it to me and I'll tailor a treatment to help you,'" Fidelino says.

An estimated 500,000 pharmaceutical trademarks are registered worldwide, and more than 15,000 prescription drugs in the United States. Over the past decade, as branding has emerged as perhaps the most critical factor affecting corporate revenues, marketing of drugs has changed vastly. It typically costs a pharmaceutical firm around $100 million to market a new drug. The change in direct-to-consumer marketing led to a big shift in the communications that surround pharmaceutical drugs. It also made these drugs a lot more like other brands. Now, when patients go to their doctors they are often aware of at least one brand-name drug that treats their dilemma—and they often request this drug by name. The shift from doctor-directed to patient-requested prescribing has meant that drugs are now a lot more like the products people encounter in their daily lives. And the names reflect this; as patients instead of doctors have become a major part of the target market, names have become less scientific sounding. The day when people reach for a drug to treat mood swings with the same level of ease they reach for a soft drink may not be too far off.

Branding in the pharmaceutical industry has suffered a fair amount of backlash—the feeling that in launching drugs there is more of a focus on brand awareness than on clinical superiority. Although drugs have a lot more serious consequences riding on them than do cars, perfumes, or handbags, like those products many drugs are still branded to sell above all else. With an increase in branding in the pharmaceutical industry, there has been a focus on differentiation in brand even when the clinical differences are minor or even nonexistent.

Each year the FDA rates the top U.S. drugs in terms of sales. An "A" rating indicates that the drug offers important therapeutic gains over existing therapies; a "B" indicates that the drug offers modest therapeutic gains over existing therapies; and a "C" indicates that the drug is considered to offer little or no therapeutic benefit over existing therapies. In recent years there have been few "A" ratings in the top-selling drugs, proving that marketing works—that consumers, both patients and doctors, are more drawn to the marketing of drugs than captivated by how well they actually work. Schering-Plough's Claritin, advertised as an improvement in allergy treatment, has sold well despite some criticism that it does not actually reduce drowsiness as much as claimed. This also shows what a number of people in the industry told me is a generalized move in the field to focus advertising less on clinical superiority than on brand awareness.

In appealing to consumers as well as doctors, pharmaceutical brands face a unique concern. If a drug does not sound medicinal, it may promote unsafe use of the drug, but sounding like a typical branded product reduces the drug's seriousness—in other words, if a name does not sound medicinal, physicians will not prescribe it. Names have to strike a balance. *Exelon* and *Lexxel,* though drug names, could really be car names. "It is important to remember that the brand name, while needing to appeal to the end-user, also needs to have a sense of gravitas and credibility with the medical profession," writes one of Fidelino's colleagues in an industry text published by Wood's corporate owner, Interbrand.

The word almost has to parrot the precise, organized system of language of the medical community with its Latin roots and identifiable prefixes and suffixes. In appealing to doctors, the names have to sound more like the generic and chemical names. And names have to dip into the more fanciful bucket of words that consumers are more keen on, filled with allusions and associations that would play to them.

Historically, when most drugs first have been introduced, they have focused on the nuts and bolts of a condition. As the drugs have evolved into second- and third-generation drug compounds, they have become more refined, with fewer side effects. As improvements and newcomers enter the marketplace, each goes further along a spectrum from nuts and bolts to emotion, from the concrete to the abstract. Dealing with hope and joy is the abstract approach, says Fidelino. "Nuts and bolts have typically driven this industry," says Fidelino. "A lot of the challenges that we face in pharmaceutical branding today is how to move the industry away from that expectation." And the way drug companies refer to new drugs backs this up. Describing Botox as a neuromuscular blocking agent or Zithromax as a macrolide antibiotic are concrete scientific approaches. Talking about Botox as a forehead-crease and crow's-foot remover and Zithromax as a powerful treatment for community-acquired pneumonia are more abstract.

"There are many instances of true innovation where they've gone straight to the abstract. And that's very wise. Because then you own the potential that any future drug would try to capture on the heels of your marketing efforts. You own not just what your one drug can do, you own the space." Fidelino mentions two Wood classics, *Viagra* and *Celebrex*. "Both of these names and their branding efforts went straight for the abstract. And so it makes it very, very difficult for newcomers to try to one-up them in that realm of relevance to human concerns." But to *own* the space, you have to *know* the space.

At Wood Worldwide a focus group is a "brandshop," a language experiment from which to test hypotheses, glean words and word parts, distill prejudices and beliefs—to see what the other side is thinking. You record the meeting and then later sit back and slice and dice the data and build a picture of what the people think and where the new message is best placed. If you learn that the doctors have trouble believing in a clinical advance, you have to break it to them the right way.

The Target Market

The purpose of a brandshop is to extract insights from two target audiences: patients and doctors. Wood typically brings in primary-care physicians as well as specialists (cardiologists, neurologists, psychologists, etc.). Sometimes U.S. doctors are joined by doctors from the European Union. Brandshops are geared to exploration or to gaining insights from the target audiences, or are validation workshops that test familiarity with existing themes and ideas and isolate the essential language for brand-name development. For a validation brandshop concerning cholesterol, for example, Wood Worldwide would want to understand the target audience's familiarity with the words used in cholesterol treatment—terms like *LDL, HDL, good cholesterol,* and *bad cholesterol.* Some validation meetings even test specific names.

Exploration meetings help Fidelino and his team to understand the concepts that drive the market. Validation meetings help them confirm whether their ideas, their "brand concepts," are correct. Such concepts can vary from the positioning of a drug as having none of the well-known side effects to another that markets a drug as providing a quicker response time. "What you want," says Fidelino, "is for the market to believe." Brand concepts, he says, are the way you want the audience to perceive the brand in a preconditioned market—that is, in a market that thinks a certain way. Brand concepts are ways to view advertising strategy. Often other outside consulting groups examine the state of the preconditioned market prior to Wood Worldwide's work. The name they create will then condition the market to believe something. If a stigma of dysfunction is associated with a certain ailment, then the name might divorce this dysfunction from its stigma. One technique could be to steal market share from an existing drug; another would be to shift market expectations completely. By testing various brand concepts and then redefining menstrual cramps as a "woman's problem," Midol was able to appeal to a larger audience. By creating a new disease category, "social anxiety disorder," or SAD, Wyeth Labs was able to sell more of its antidepressant Effexor.

In the early stages of developing a new drug name, Fidelino

and his team find it useful to evaluate the current lexicon that surrounds the particular drug space. For them, a focus group of doctors is a living language laboratory, where they can gauge the talk value of current words and distill the perceptions doctors have of certain drugs that the new concept will vie against.

After six o'clock at night, the offices of Wood Worldwide have pretty much cleared out, except for Fidelino and his team. The adults are gone, letting the kids roam free. As night falls, they set up the conference room and take a dry run through the program for the meeting that evening. They will host twelve neurologists for an hour and a half to discuss the landscape of a particular condition and the idea for a new drug that will someday fit into that landscape.

Wood Worldwide's offices occupy almost a whole floor of a stylish building in Manhattan's SoHo district. The casually well-dressed workers operate Apple iMacs and sit in ergonomically sound Herman Miller Aeron chairs, covered in trademarked black Pellicle fabric (brands that largely defined the workplace culture of the New Economy). In the months after Interbrand bought Wood Worldwide, the firm expanded by knocking out some walls and hiring an interior decorator to update the firm's already futuristic aesthetic. Just inside the entry doors there is a large, multi-sided glass meeting room decked out in gray sound-dampening foam. The room is wired with the latest audiovisual equipment that can record and transmit meetings. Places like Wood have a vested interest in projecting an image to convey that they are in touch with the future—like a corporate Tomorrowland. When they visit Wood, both doctors and clients are made to feel as if they've left their own quotidian, present-day worlds.

The doctors who show up for the after-hours gathering with Fidelino's young, pop-culture-attuned staff could easily get a sense that they have entered a screening room at MTV. They're a fairly homogeneous group—a handful of Russians, one Asian man, and just one woman doctor. There are a couple of mustaches, some beards, a lot of suits and ties. In front of the room, Fidelino wears a blue sweater that hangs over rustic rawhide leather pants, and he sports black work boots. He welcomes the group and tells them that tonight they'll be helping to provide information and understanding about the pharmaceutical treatment of a debilitating disease that hampers daily life.

"Allow yourself to be real people, not just doctors," Fidelino says as he begins the workshop.

Fidelino asks the physicians to discuss all of the brands in their world—the names of drugs they prescribe. Based on their in-depth descriptions, it became clear to me that physicians were largely at the mercy of the pharmaceutical companies. And these doctors are largely restrained in treating patients by the drugs that they can prescribe, by the limitations of the drugs that are manufactured. Very literally, the treatment nowadays is out of their hands. Yet these doctors are also averse to the notion of branding—it's clear that it's beneath them to prescribe something that is clearly branded. It goes against their grain to feel manipulated by a pharmaceutical giant, after all their years in medical school. Part of Fidelino's job is to determine just how averse the doctors are to the marketing messages they have been showered with, to better position his client in their minds.

Because every day they face patients with real, incapacitating conditions, these doctors are living in the present, while Fidelino and team are, if not actually living in the future, spending a lot of time thinking about it. "I know you are going to think this is too good to be true," says Fidelino as he hands out a product description of a new pill to the roomful of doctors, a sort of postcard from the future. The conversation among the doctors very quickly turns remarkably complex as the doctors heatedly discuss what has been unveiled in front of them. Some simply are not convinced, others are intrigued.

Over the course of the meeting, I sense a growing hostility by a couple of doctors toward Fidelino and his crew, most of whom quietly hand out and collect worksheets or take notes. But during this most medical phase, Fidelino and his team have an impressive ability to follow the doctors' discussion as it plunges into technical medical science relating to cellular structures and DNA molecules. And through this show of smarts, a leveling of attitudes seems to transpire.

Toward the meeting's end, the doctors have been split into groups of three and instructed to choose magazine cutout images that match the specific pills that they prescribe for various predicaments.

One guy asks, "Do you think that we'll all pick the same pictures?" The lone woman doctor answers, "Statistically it's very unlikely."

"If you could design your own ad, what would you do?" asks Fidelino.

He presents four options: *smooth, high performance, optimization,* and *simplicity.* The high-performance concept, in particular, leaves some doctors stunned. Images of cheetahs jumping through flames seem to mock the disease they treat. One sarcastic doctor offers that the high-performance concept would work better for advertising MDMA, the drug compound informally known as Ecstasy. It's clear that Fidelino has pushed them to a place where they don't feel comfortable. By meeting's end, despite a few fleeting tensions, Fidelino has harvested a good crop of data that will allow Wood to position the next drug name in the minds of these specialists.

Viagra, n.

Founded in 1849, Pfizer is arguably the most powerful pharmaceutical company in the world. More than 165 million people worldwide take Pfizer medications, and in 2002, the company had eight products in its portfolio that racked up sales of more than $1 billion each and was one of the top ten companies in terms of profits. In 1999, Pfizer conducted a successful hostile takeover of Warner-Lambert, a company with which it had co-marketed the cholesterol-lowering drug Lipitor since 1996. Pfizer wanted to add Lipitor to its own exclusive portfolio. In 2001, Lipitor became the best-selling drug in the world. In 2003, for $57 billion, Pfizer acquired rival Pharmacia, a firm with which it had co-promoted the arthritis drug Celebrex. In the pharmaceutical industry, there's Pfizer and then everyone else. The company's bold-sounding motto is "Life Is Our Life's Work." In 2003, Pfizer spent a whopping $7.1 billion on research—the hunt for new pills.

In the late 1980s, Pfizer research scientists working at the company labs in Sandwich, England, discovered a series of pyrazolopyrimidinone compounds to treat such heart problems as angina pectoris, a chest pain caused by a sudden decrease in blood supply to the heart muscle. One particular series of this compound, sildenafil citrate, was patented in 1991, and the patent included a claim for its use as a heart medicine. In 1992, during trial studies of sildenafil as a heart medicine, Pfizer scientists found that it also increased blood flow to the penis. Further directed studies showed that the scientists had stumbled on a possible cure for male impotence—the inability to maintain an erection, and the associated inability to engage in sexual intercourse. With major implications at stake, scientists at Pfizer eagerly worked out a nine-step process to synthesize a sildenafil compound into a pill.

Unlike other pharmaceutical treatments for impotence, the new compound did not directly cause penile erections but affected the response to sexual arousal. The drug acted by enhancing the release of nitric oxide, a chemical normally released in response to sexual stimulation, and led to smooth-muscle relaxation. The new drug also inhibited an enzyme called PDE-5, relaxing the smooth-muscle cells in the penis, thus enabling blood to flow in and create an erection.

There were few effective treatments for impotence in the early 1990s, and most shared less than ideal application procedures, such as a self-administered injection into the urethra called Muse, manufactured by a small group called Vivus, and a similar Upjohn product named Caverject. The names were clearly an attempt to show their worth to patients—*Muse* alluded to outside assistance, *Caverject* was a much more direct and less glossy allusion to the area being injected (corpora cavernosa). That some men were willing to inject themselves with the drugs showed a clear demand—impotence was a problem crying out for a simple oral treatment.

Having stumbled onto a possible answer to a problem faced by an estimated 13 million men in the United States alone, Pfizer moved the drug immediately forward into clinical trials. By 1997, the trial compound was evaluated in numerous random, placebo-controlled trials involving more than four thousand men with varying degrees of impotence associated with diabetes, spinal cord injury, history of prostate surgery, or no identifiable underlying physical cause. Patients also had a wide range of other concomitant illnesses, including hypertension and coronary artery disease. Patients who participated in the tests kept diaries of their sexual histories to help researchers.

In parallel with the battery of lab exercises that Pfizer executed to prove the efficacy of the new pill, the company also, in early trial stages, turned to the marketing issues that would surround the launch of a potential drug. If all tests went well, a drug that effectively and easily treated impotence—a breakthrough drug with a multimillion-man market—could be worth *billions* of dollars. But efficacy was only a part of the battle.

Years before Pfizer had any assurance that the trial impotence drug would gain regulatory approval, the scientists at Pfizer painted a picture for the team at Wood Worldwide of a future world where a simple pill would allow an impotent man to engage normally in sex. David Wood and his team had to learn a lot about the landscape—how men dealt with impotence.

Wood Worldwide quickly called together several exploratory focus groups to examine impotence, to dig deeper into the problem and find out how patients who suffered from impotence felt about themselves, and to gain an overview of the linguistic landscape of the condition from a doctor's and a patient's perspective. It was immediately clear to David Wood and his colleagues that impotence was something that deeply troubled the people who suffered from it, to the point that just talking about it was difficult. It was tricky to get people in off the streets to discuss the subject, even in paid focus groups. They were dealing with a stigmatized condition—but one that Wood and Pfizer had a shot at destigmatizing. This was where the group excelled: in crafting new words and substituting new pieces of language for others that no longer served a purpose.

It took Wood's researchers some trial and error before they filled focus groups with impotent men who were comfortable discussing their problems. "Once the barriers came down, a club developed," remembers David Wood. "At that moment in time, it was the most stigmatizing condition for men, the ultimate kick in the chops." The reticence that men had in sharing—and their subsequent relief in chatting about impotence—suggested to the team at Wood Worldwide that they needed to very carefully find a way to allow men to talk about the condition, and they set about shifting the name for the condition called impotence.

The name itself was a loaded term that suggested a lack of power, feebleness, frailty, exhaustion, weakness, ineffectiveness—*not potent*. Wood Worldwide also had to move the associations from smut to medicine. Early names for the drug that came out of creative work at Wood tended to sound like condoms—variations on words like *Hercules* and *Trojan*. This was the obvious, expected, banal work, according to David Wood. But when men were asked what they would be like after they ate a pill, they talked about forces of nature.

Let the Dance Begin

Tom Ruth, assistant director of new-product development at Pfizer, spends 80 percent of his time dealing with naming. Ruth is no wild-eyed dreamer but a down-to-earth pragmatist charged with a key aspect of his company's marketing. In the original conception, he concedes, the impotence pill was going to have a discreet name. "When your friends came over and opened up your medicine cabinet," he says, "they would have no idea what you were taking." That, he admits, was a very early-1990s idea. And not what Wood had in mind.

When Wood Worldwide presents names to clients, it is the first time that the story is told. Based on the focus-group feedback, Wood's creative team brainstormed words and word parts. Fidelino likes to present between thirty and fifty names to clients after the creative work is completed. He often presents names in the context of advertisements, pills shown stamped with the various names. "Context is important," Fidelino says. "Otherwise, names don't have resonance." Wood Worldwide's clients have to be on board, they have to get excited, or a name won't work out. With the impotence pill, *vi-* came to stand in for *vitality* and *vigor*, with *virility* as a key word root. *Agra* is a word-part meaning "catch" or "grasp." With the condition recast as "erectile dysfunction," the brand name for Pfizer's miracle drug could gain a fertile foothold to spring from. Once the name was settled on, *Viagra,* it still had to enter into dialogue between men and themselves, between men and their partners. *Viagra* had to join a conversation about impotence—or better yet, lead one about erectile dysfunction.

Fidelino tells his clients not to Rohrschach—don't look at a name like *Viagra* and think *Niagara* (that massive waterfall and once-famous newlywed destination). "Just take the word at face value," he says. "Ask yourself 'What potential does this name have to support your message?' " To Fidelino, the degree to which you can imbue a word with meaning is called "vesting." And Viagra was about to be heavily vested.

Viagra had the feeling of an older name, one that called to mind Italian frescoes and the marketplace—the Greek *agora*. It is not jarring but familiar-sounding, in the same way that the scents imbued in fabric softeners can make one subconsciously comprehend a springtime field of flowers that one has never actually seen or smelled. It's a subtle name, maybe that of a space-age aphrodisiac dropped off on Earth by a set of roving aliens. It's a Trojan horse of words, ready to disgorge meaning if necessary. If you run Viagra through a Lexicon test, matching it to other powerful and enhancing products, it does well. Indeed, most products want to be powerful, easy to use, and friendly. A *Viagra* race car? Yes. A *Viagra* high-altitude helicopter? Indeed. A set of all-terrain running shoes? Absolutely. These associations would allow *Viagra the name* to develop into *Viagra the narrative*.

The trade dress for the pill would be blue and diamond-shaped. In pharmaceutical marketing, more concern is paid to the color, shape, and size of a pill than most people realize as a way to increase the product's differentiation. Unique size and coloration can help patients distinguish one pill from another and also influence consumer preferences. Round white pills no longer cut it in a world of two-tone capsules and neon-pink tablets. Merck's Prilosec, the ulcer medication, was marketed heavily as "the purple pill," in a sophisticated attempt to build consumer loyalty around a color that could serve as a bridge to a new Merck treatment.

Pfizer's "erectile dysfunction" pill, having proceeded through regulatory approval, was approved by the FDA on March 27, 1998, and launched on April 10. Viagra was the first pill to treat impotence. By June of that year, 2.7 million prescriptions were filled and $411 million in sales were recorded. The next year Pfizer sold more than $1 billion worth of Viagra. Behind massive sales was a large marketing campaign augmented by widespread word of mouth. Sales of Viagra in 2002 totaled $1.7 billion, an increase of 14 percent from the year before. This was no fluke of marketing, no accident.

Bob Dole, a U.S. senator from Kansas and presidential candidate, took part in a clinical trial for the compound and in May 1998 mentioned to Larry King how much it had helped him after prostate cancer surgery. Pfizer later asked Dole to take part in a perception-altering campaign. It was a move that changed drug marketing. Dole served as a spokesman for the disease that soon came to be widely known as erectile dysfunction, and urged people to see their physicians. His role helped Viagra gain major talk value and the ultimate test of currency: appearance in TV comedy routines.

Because word of mouth and personal testimonials are recognized as sales drivers, some of the most effective drug recommendations come from personalities whom customers respect. By endorsing Viagra (shortly after losing the presidential race),

Bob Dole stepped into new territory. Other drugmakers have made use of well-known user-endorsers: Nolan Ryan (Alleve), Joan Lunden (Claritin), and Lance Armstrong (Bristol-Myers Squibb cancer treatments).

In 2001, as Viagra was known throughout the civilized world, NASCAR driver Mark Martin assumed the position as driver of the Viagra car in the Winston Cup Series and as a spokesman for men's health. The 2001 Earth, Wind & Fire Cool Blue Summer Tour was heavily sponsored by Viagra as a part of the Viagra Concert Series. Advertisements encouraged concertgoers to come to a Pfizer booth: "Health can often be measured in numbers. Why not get yours checked?" In 2001, baseball player Rafael Palmeiro signed on as a second user-spokesman. By 2002, Pfizer reported that 44 million prescriptions had been written for the drug and that more than 13 million men in the world had "rediscover[ed] their love lives."

To some, Viagra's Achilles' heel was that it did not immediately start working upon ingestion, and this factor led to a leveling off in what were once astronomical sales. Even into 2001, Pfizer was spending more than $90 million per year in advertising the blue, diamond-shaped pills. Viagra soon encountered its first competition from Eli Lilly, whose Cialis impotence drug launched in the U.S. market in 2003. Jointly, GlaxoSmithKline and Bayer AG came out with Levitra. Both drugs claimed they worked faster and lasted longer than Viagra and had fewer side effects based on an ability to block the enzyme PDE-5 more selectively, requiring smaller doses and interacting with fewer molecules. These names were no great leaps, even if the drugs had some superior clinical aspects. *Cialis* gave users little to go on in terms of name interpretation, whereas *Levitra* contained a *Viagra*-like *vi* word part and a connection to levitation.

Not long after its release to treat what is a serious condition for some people, Viagra found its way into recreational use. In San Francisco, where one street name had Viagra as "Vitamin V" or simply "the blue pill," the city's director of sexually transmitted disease prevention made it his mission to ask Pfizer to label its product more clearly with a warning that its use could lead to unsafe sex practices.

Viagra was such a clinical advance that it could have been named something less powerful. A great product reflects well on a mediocre name. At one point, with his guard down, Fidelino mentioned offhandedly that Viagra had actually been a name developed for another drug—a treatment of some sort for the kidney. Like BlackBerry, the right name existed before the product. The two together—the groundbreaking pill and the life-affirming name—made history.

Viagra exemplifies the rapid insertion of a coined name into public consciousness. Wood Worldwide faced the challenge of developing and presenting a brand name that would gain global visibility while eliminating the stigma attached to the drug's category. With a coined name that avoided the traditional pharmaceutical brand-name look and feel, and through a marketing push that evoked wellness and suggested benefits, Viagra hit the mark. American society was soon in the sway of Viagra. The drug became a touchstone of baby-boomer conversations, a savior of marriages.

Next up for Pfizer would be, among others, Relpax, an oral treatment for migraine headaches touted as the next billion-dollar drug and named by Wood. "*Relpax* is a great name," Pfizer's Ruth told me, "in large part because it is different from the other drugs out there—like *Zomig* and *Imigran*." To Ruth the word *Relpax* says *relief* and *peace of mind*. "It's a fast word that has the words *relief* and *peace* (*pax*) inside it." Relpax first met approval in Europe and Japan, where it had 2002 sales of $16 million; similar sales would follow in the United States after late-2002 approval. Relpax certainly staked out the more conceptual zone than its relatives Zomig and Imigran, stuck as they were in an older era of pharmaceutical names and with roots closer to migraine. *Rel + pax* = real peace, an abstract idea that would deeply resonate with anyone who had ever had a migraine.

Amazing Literary Viagra

As for the one pharmaceutical name that I had consulted on briefly, for Glaxo Wellcome, it was launched in 2000 as *Trizivir* (a name that spoke to the three-in-one nature of the compound and positioned the new drug close to another Glaxo drug, Combivir). The placards appeared on bus shelters in San Francisco—the ad campaign we had modeled in our presentation. The name was not far from some of the ones Glasgow and I had created—*Synthrivir* and *Triumvir* had been our favorites. Just two letters (and thousands of dollars and man-hours) separated ours from the winning choice. We, of course, really had little chance to name that drug. We were not well versed in the particularities of naming drugs: the many competing problems each drug's name must resolve, from FDA regulations to changing consumer sentiments. We had been more the poets in that situation than qualified brand advisers, the far-left-field group brought in to spice up the mix of stalwart firms with track records in the pharmaceutical industry.

Viagra was more of an idea than a pill when it emerged as a character in a novel and was placed in the leading English-language dictionary. Both were dreams come true for marketers, practitioners of wordcraft. To David Wood, "the ultimate global shorthand" was indeed that; although birthed through synthetic means, *Viagra* was a word with plenty of meaning. It found its way into a novel by none other than Philip Roth, the author who had written famously, and provocatively, about masturbation in his widely read third novel, *Portnoy's Complaint.*

In Roth's PEN/Faulkner Award–winning novel *The Human Stain,* he tells the story of an aging college professor embroiled in a campus love affair with a younger woman. "I owe all of this turbulence and happiness to Viagra," the professor tells his confidante. "Without Viagra none of this would be happening. Without Viagra I would have a picture of the world appropriate to my age and wholly different aims. Without Viagra I would have the dignity of an elderly gentleman free from desire who behaves correctly. I would not be doing something unseemly, rash, ill-considered, and potentially disastrous to all involved. Without Viagra, I would continue, in my declining years, to develop the broad impersonal perspective of an experienced and educated honorably discharged man who has long ago given up the sensual enjoyment of life. I could continue to draw profound philosophical conclusions and have a steadying moral influence on the young, instead of having put myself back into the perpetual state of emergency that is sexual intoxication. Thanks to Viagra I've come to understand Zeus's amorous transformations. That's what they should have called Viagra. They should have called it Zeus."

Through this character, Roth examined the role of Viagra in particular and the abundance of lifestyle drugs in general. Some of these drugs have obvious and serious medical uses that few would question. Others seem to attempt to banish all discomforts that we as humans face, and to cover up all imperfections in our appearance and hide the inevitable ravages of aging. Viagra had indeed staked out the future and swayed the thoughts and actions of characters both real and fictional.

Because of the limited time it has to own the market, the bigger a brand name Viagra had going forward, the more market share it could own. And even as other solutions followed Viagra to market, its name would make people trust it as the first name, the gold standard in dealing with impotence. And Pfizer will make changes, tweak the drug over time so that consumers will always turn to Viagra whenever they have needs in the sex department. That's why David Wood wants Pfizer to sponsor a clothing line or a Valentine's Day parade—to further associate that word, *Viagra,* with love and sex.

In China, where men have long self-medicated themselves with a range of aphrodisiacs drawn from seal, cattle, sheep, sea lion, dog, and deer penises, Viagra became a hot item as soon as it was approved for sale in 2000 and was even found in counterfeit form before then. In China the word *Viagra* was transliterated, meaning that words, characters, and sounds in Chinese were used that closely resembled the word written in the Roman alphabet. To many in China the name became *Wanaige* (using characters for "sex," "pill," and "love"), and many people called it by a nickname, *weige* (pronounced *way-guh*), which means "great elder brother." China, the land of the aphrodisiac, where sexual sciences had long been practiced, proved an interesting mirror, reflecting back brand messages telegraphed from the United States. The Chinese word sounded loosely like *Viagra,* but its meaning was far different. *Viagra* (or *weige*) was the newest addition to the medicine man's bag of tricks. In China, too, the *name* would be the thing with the most power, after all. And the name would either be a foreign name or simply the great elder brother—a source of great assistance in all matters sexual and an aphrodisiac that arouses or increases sexual desire.

According to Pfizer, far less real product had been sent to China than appeared to be sold in stores. Either crafty manufacturers had brewed up their own batches of blue pills or there were placebos floating around, not perhaps that different from other aphrodisiacs of questionable power and potency—the great elder brothers, as it were. The placebo effect might show that patients, consumers, care about the messaging that surrounds a pill—that the words have their own healing effect. That the *promise* inherent in a brand name might even influence its efficacy.

Someday the pharmaceutical field could be shifted entirely toward a more traditional sphere of branding—where each firm is known for solving one set of problems, for addressing certain consumer wants and needs. Viagra could be a spin-off company or a renamed Pfizer that offers consumers answers to love and sex (parades, singles bars, birth control, etc.) in the way that Coca-Cola meets people's refreshment needs. Prozac could do the same, offering a full range of mental-health services from specially trained therapists to relaxing weekend getaways.

Because drug names now reach for an abstract and seek to own great swaths of the consumer mind, these intangible and synthetic compounds are the area of branded products that is most poetry-like in nature. Just as poems pack grand amounts of meaning into few words through detail and summation, so, too, do drug names. They are created in a crucible, the best ones distilled down to the rudiments of letters and word parts able to convey meaning.

According to the *OED*, *Viagra* was a "proprietary name for: the drug sildenafil citrate, given orally in the treatment of male impotence. Also *fig.*" Dictionary citations included the first mention from a press release: "Viagra, for male erectile dysfunction." And a later figurative mention from Stephen King's *On Writing*: "The effect of judicious cutting is immediate and often amazing literary Viagra."

In the end, all drug names want to reach the marketing nirvana that Viagra did. With a limited number of years to sell, the drug reached a critical mass, and as an idea, not simply a name, it spread. And it spread organically, from patient to patient, doctor to doctor, husband to wife, partner to partner. *Viagra*—a made-up word that gained a following, that gained *fans,* as David Wood would have it. And Wood, it seemed, was, if not beating the fiction writers at their own game, at least staying a step ahead.

GETTING THE
WORD OUT

8

It should be clear by now that creating a word is just a start. The word must then be launched, projected, emitted, transferred—sent out into orbit. In choosing and then broadcasting a name, one can turn to either top-down or bottom-up techniques. In a top-down scenario, you start by creating a name that is distinctly protectable, a fanciful name like *Accenture*. To do this on a massive scale is extremely expensive, because the word you end up with is typically not very closely tied in meaning to the product or service. *Accenture* (or *Vivendi* or *Verizon*) does not overtly say anything about what the company does—one needs to be indoctrinated to learn what this term means. In a bottom-up scenario, on the other hand, a name is created and launched with the idea that future customers will be willing participants in the word's spread. Instead of being manufactured with a built-in need to educate people, these words are geared to natural proliferation. These two flip sides of the coin often compete with each other in the marketplace.

A classic example of the free and easy movement of words and related success in the marketplace was Budweiser's wildly popular *Whassup!* campaign. Launched on Christmas Day 1999, and then aired to a larger audience during the 2000 Super Bowl, the *Whassup!* ad campaign was fairly simple. Each of the television ads featured a group of friends who call one another on the telephone. The caller says "Whassup?" to the friend he is calling, and those two friends call another friend. With each call, the greeting gets drawn out more and more, until it's a long drawn-out "Whassssuuuupppp?" The answer to the question of "Whassup?" comes out casually. "I'm just sitting here, drinking a Bud."

The campaign did not begin in an ad agency but as a short film directed by Charles Stone III. Stone made the film as a calling card, a way to try to land a job as a director of a feature film. It caught the attention of the creative team at the ad agency DDB, which was creating a new advertising campaign for its client Anheuser-Busch. According to DDB, the ads were not really about Budweiser beer at all. These were ads about male bonding. They were also a platform to launch a word into the world tied to Budweiser.

After the first seven ads aired on TV, more and more people found themselves using the word to greet one another like the characters in the ads. The word *Whassup!* found its way onto late-night television shows. Imitation versions of the ads sprang up on the Internet. "Other traditional advertisers might have seen these *Whassup!* ripoffs and said 'cease and desist,'" Bob Lachky, Anheuser-Busch's vice president for brand management, told the *New York Times*. "But we said, 'Stop? What, are you crazy? This is great, this idea is cool, and Bud is an integral part of it.'" Lachky credited the Internet for spreading the word. It was something he admitted you could never truly plan, and luck had a good deal to do with the success.

Bob Scarpelli, DDB's chief creative officer in the United States and creative director behind the *Whassup!* campaign, says the Bud commercials had "talk value," another way to describe the creation of buzz—an intangible quality that, when married with a requisite amount of media exposure, begins to seep into the culture. Planning the spread of ideas into the original equation, DDB, and other firms, think about this more and more, and effective understanding of the methods with which words and ideas enter the vernacular can heavily influence the success or failure of a campaign. The *Whassup!* campaign won numerous industry awards. DDB would later estimate that *Whassup!*'s talk value had generated some $20 million in free advertising.

Anheuser-Busch appropriated the term *Whassup!* from popular (and more specifically African-American) culture, and directly from Stone's videotape. With great advertising, it was deftly spun back out into a wider popular audience with an added asterisk of recognition—the brand name of Budweiser. Like the piece of modern slang that it was, *Whassup!* paralleled the friend-to-friend and office-mate to office-mate spread of slang words (*bitchin',* *radical, slammin', the bomb*) that come and go with the times. (To some, it should be noted, this was not such a great thing—their greeting had been co-opted and taken away for good.) Anheuser-Busch did register *Whassup!* as a trademark, but, as Lachky makes clear, the company did not patrol its use. Not every marketer behind the launch of a new brand name can be so laissez-faire about ownership as Anheuser-Busch was. But still, *Whassup!* serves as a great model for the future spread of ideas. *Whassup!* was a free-range idea, a maverick.

There are at least two reasons why *Whassup!* worked so well. First, the ads were funny and the word was easy to imitate—everywhere it spread, it grew through imitation. Second, saying *Whassup!* proved to be fun. Everyone did it, from TV actors to the guy in the cubicle next door. Creating a word that others will copy is vital. Something copied like this has been called a *meme*. Memes can be ideas, words, and facial expressions—anything that can be reproduced and passed along. And like plants and animals, these ideas evolve. (Anheuser-Bush even created its own ad spin-offs that promoted this evolution, like one playing on the word *wasabi* as a stand-in for *Whassup!*)

In fact, the word *meme* was first conceived by Oxford biologist Richard Dawkins in his book *The Selfish Gene*. Dawkins believed that when we imitate someone, something is passed on, and he called that element a *meme*. The word itself took off, finding its way into the *Oxford English Dictionary*, which defines it as "an element of culture that may be considered to be passed on by nongenetic means, especially imitation." Some contend, as Oxford professor Susan Blackmore does, that language is related to evolution and that the origin and subsequent spread and use of language is a means of survival. Whether the spread of language is a part of evolution remains under debate in academic circles, but there is little doubt that language spreads in unique ways. Drilling down into everyday, modern uses of language, Blackmore shows in her book *The Meme Machine* that certain words and parts of language spread more widely than others.

Viagra was a meme well suited to spread. "Memes that deal with sex, food, and power all press powerful meme 'buttons' because of the importance of these topics in our evolutionary past," writes Blackmore. "Another way of putting it is that genetic evolution has created brains that are especially concerned with sex, food, and power, and the memes we 'choose' reflect those genetic concerns."

By making sure that words are pronounceable, naming firms make it easier for words to move into the cultural slipstream. At its best, some travel capacity should be hardwired into a name. BlackBerry, as we saw earlier, is easy to pronounce and memorable—two features that helped drive sales of the email pager. In the world of idea generation and dissemination, if you can harness the "memetic" nature of something, and make it more likely to be passed along, you will do better than your competitor in the marketplace of ideas.

When Stanford business school professor Chip Heath first asked his MBA students why the *Whassup!* ad campaign had been so successful, they gave him what he considered to be a standard answer—that the ad campaign did a good job of targeting the right demographic audience. But Heath believes that Anheuser-Busch had maximized the environmental cues for people and made it easier to use the word in everyday speech. Because "Whassup!" is a salutation, which is a part of speech we all use every day, Anheuser-Busch was able to insert its brand of beer more easily into this exchange. People who said "Whassup!" instead of "Hello" were advertising Budweiser to one another. Heath points to the "Where's the beef?" ad campaign created by ad agency Dancer Fitzgerald Sample for Wendy's that aired in the late 1980s. In a similar fashion, he says, people readily adopted that slogan because it dealt with an issue often faced in the real world—lack of substance—as in "Where's the story, where's the real meat?" The slogan became a tool, an expression they could use.

"Where's the beef?," like "Got Milk?" a decade later, referred to the products that they were advertising. Both were successful campaigns. And Anheuser-Busch's "This Bud's for You" and "Weekends Were Made for Michelob" slogans had long done the same. "Whassup!" referred to Budweiser in a less linear fashion, invoking only tangentially things like male bonding and beer drinking. But their ubiquity ensured converts in a way that some tightly constrained words did not.

Top-Down Naming at Mile High

Sponsoring a large public entity—like a football stadium—is a tried-and-true way to get brand recognition, to boost talk value and launch a word into a wider trajectory. When a company pays to put its name on a stadium, that name will gain entry into many places, inserting itself as a micro-advertisement and inevitably swaying minds.

Stadiums have been known by corporate monikers ever since William Wrigley and August Busch put their names on fields used by the teams they owned. The modern era of commercial names truly started in 1973, when Rich Foods paid $1.5 million to put its name on the home of football's Buffalo Bills for twenty-five years. Fifteen years later, Atlantic Richfield and Great Western Financial Corporation put their names on basketball arenas in Sacramento (Arco Arena) and Los Angeles (Great Western Forum). According to Dean Bonham, a naming-rights consultant in Denver, Colorado, by 2002, sixty-two major-league stadiums sported the names of companies, and those companies had agreed to pay a collective $3.4 billion for the privilege over as long as thirty years.

Most stadiums are built with tax dollars, so selling naming rights can be a prickly subject with citizens who rightly contend that they should have some say in what their local stadium is named. Denver, Colorado, was the site of a hearty protest in 2001. For me it was a way to see top-down naming in progress, to view the power and meaning of a word through the eyes of the people who would use it every day, and to witness a war of words playing out in the thin Rocky Mountain air.

The fifteenth step on the west side of the state capitol building in Denver is 5,280 feet (1,609 meters) above sea level. People started calling Denver "the mile-high city" in the 1950s when

I. M. Pei designed the Mile High Center, a twenty-three-story office tower at 17th and Broadway. The name spoke for the people of Denver and gave them a sense of pride and place. Mile High came to say to Denver residents that they stood in possession of 5,280 feet of vertical space over their sea-level neighbors of the Midwest flatlands. Soon it became the name of the stadium where the Broncos football squad intimidated rivals at the high altitude.

In 2001, a new Mile High Stadium was being built, and the team's owners managed to sell the naming rights for $120 million to a local financial corporation. What was once Mile High Stadium would soon become the clunky, unwieldy *Invesco Field at Mile High*. As I planned my trip to Denver, I was acutely aware of how people I talked to spoke of the new stadium and how I referred to it. I knew, and everyone else knew as well, that Mile High as a name would soon fade away. The new name would emerge and take its place.

To arrange for a press pass to a Broncos game in the new stadium, I called the press relations head, a jovial guy named Jim Saccomano. In conversations leading up to the game, Saccomano made it clear to me that nobody he knew was referring to the old name or shortening, altering, or abbreviating the new name in any way. "It would be like calling Muhammad Ali Cassius Clay," he told me with conviction.

When I landed at the airport in Denver, a lighted sign told me to "Enjoy Our Mile High Experience." I checked into my hotel and found a magazine called *5280: Denver's Mile-High Magazine*. Already, I saw that the name *Mile High* had permeated deeply. I was in the Mile High City to watch the Denver Broncos play the Seattle Seahawks inside the fresh, new stadium. Kickoff was at 6:30 p.m., and it was a brisk but not too cold early-December night.

On my way to the game, I tested my taxi driver to find out his opinion of the name change, and to gauge the current state of interest or lack of interest in the new name around the wider Denver metropolitan area. I asked him to take me to Mile High Stadium. "It's not called 'Mile High Stadium' anymore. It's 'Invesco Field,'" he told me.

As we drove on, I trained myself to remember that the stadium had five words—Invesco . . . Field . . . at . . . Mile . . . High—and in the cab I said it to myself several times. I did not want to blunder when I talked to the Broncos' press people, who had been kind enough to grant me press credentials.

But fans were not being as careful as my driver. At the game I heard people call it "the new Mile High Stadium." Some called it simply "Mile High." I heard "Invesco Field." One guy carefully referred to the stadium as the "At Mile High."

I headed over to one of a few tailgate parties near the stadium, homing in on one that was well attended and heated by a roaring flame that leapt out from an impromptu fire pit. "Sweet Home Alabama" played loudly from the speakers of a towering four-by-four pickup. I cornered three grizzled fans who all sported beards and Wranglers. They'd been season ticket holders for more than thirty years—"South Standers," they proudly told me, referring to the cheaper bleacher seats they called home.

"I think they screwed the people of Denver," said Paul, convinced that the Broncos' owner Pat Bowlen "scurried the deal and pocketed $60 million." The three guys wondered where all the money went. "Did it reduce the deficit to the taxpayer?" asked Paul rhetorically. "I don't know. But Invesco Field? Please." Murray disagreed with Paul: "Heck, if we want to get serious, we should call it 'Bears Stadium,'" he offered, referring to the original name of Mile High.

I entered through the press door, gaining my first view directly through the North Tunnel out onto the green field, bathed under the sunlike incandescence of 1,500 kilowatts of whitish halogen lamps. I climbed the stairs four floors to the press box and sat down just in time for kickoff. It was a great game, with Denver triumphant.

One of the hosts from ESPN's *Sunday Night Football* told me that he had been instructed by ESPN management to call the stadium by its full name. When I watched a tape of the game, sure enough, ESPN's booth announcers Mike Patrick, Joe Thiesmann, and Paul Maguire signed off from Mile High Stadium, not Invesco Field.

When Invesco Funds Group decided to sponsor the new stadium in Denver, it did so in a deliberate attempt to weave its name into the language of Denver, the language that surrounds football, and the language that would be used in the media, in local papers, and in nationwide broadcasts. There are no mavericks here; the stadium-naming model is fairly predictable. Companies like Invesco rely on the shorthand that people adopt to insinuate their name into the everyday vocabulary of consumers. A football fan might head down to "Invesco Field," or simply to "Invesco," using the word as a substitute, like saying "Whassup!" instead of "How's it going?" The name gains relevance through simple repetition. This is basic, if expensive, brand building.

When they recognize that the park they've visited for years is no longer going to have the same name, coupled with the fact that the new name will be commercial, people often react negatively to these stadium sponsorships. In San Francisco, people were incredulous that they had to call Candlestick Park *3Com Park*. Candlestick Park had become an idea over time, a verbal summation of the experience of attending a San Francisco Giants or 49ers game—more often than not in windswept and foggy weather that gave sports fans a visceral perception. In Denver, the plan did not go smoothly—in large part thanks to a group of people who did not ever want to utter a commercial name in relation to their beloved stadium.

The desire to keep calling the stadium *Mile High* ran deep. In April 2000, John Hickenlooper, a local bar owner, heard from his friend Lew Cady that the Denver Broncos, after building a new stadium, planned to sell the naming rights. The old name—*Mile High Stadium*—was a vital part of the local vocabulary and an important part of Denver's cultural identity, and Cady, the creative director at a Denver ad firm, thought they should voice their opposition to the change. Cady had taken the first step, printing bumper stickers in support of the old name: "Best Name by a Mile."

Hickenlooper took his own quick poll of local sentiment, querying people seated at the bar of his flagship brewery, and found that there was almost unanimous opposition to a private entity (the Denver Broncos) selling and profiting from naming rights to a stadium built by Denver taxpayers.

Hickenlooper came to view *Mile High* as a brand name, and as something worth fighting to keep. And not only for sentimental value—Hickenlooper was convinced that the name *Mile High* had a dollar value to the city of Denver. Hickenlooper, who serves on the city's Convention and Visitors Bureau, came to think about the name through that lens—as a magnet for attracting visitors to the city. He said that every time an NFL viewer tuned in to a game from Mile High, where snow-capped peaks could often be seen, the city of Denver scored a solid piece of advertising. He geared up for a fight, and the main opposition to the name change, Friends of Mile High, was born.

Hickenlooper paid for a poll to be conducted that determined that 38 percent of Denver residents supported a name that combined a corporate name with "Mile High," while an equal number wanted to keep the name free of corporate identification. In October 2000, Hickenlooper got a call from Denver's mayor, Wellington Webb. He was interested in joining the fight and called a press conference. Friends of Mile High was now at the center of a citywide debate.

In January 2001, Rick Reilly, the well-known *Sports Illustrated* back-page columnist, rallied behind the cause. In a column titled "Corpo-Name Disease: Stop the Plague!" he described a malaise creeping through America attached to the widespread corporate naming of stadiums. He expressed a brotherhood with Hicken-looper, the "skinny restaurateur." Reilly called on the citizens of Chicago to rise up against any sort of commercial twist on the name Soldier Field, and on the citizens of Boston, whose Red Sox were rumored to be heading out of Fenway into a stadium possi-bly named Polaroid Park. At the end of his column, Reilly rallied his readers to find "the Hickenlooper inside you!"

Regardless of the opposition, the stadium builders went ahead and tried to negotiate a deal with one of several local corporate sponsors. After several potential deals fell through, including one to take sponsorship money from three companies that did not want the name to change from Mile High Stadium, the Metropolitan Football Stadium District voted on January 29, 2001, to accept a naming-rights offer from Invesco Funds Group, a Denver-based mutual funds company. Invesco purchased the naming rights to the new stadium for twenty years for a price of $60 million. Invesco also purchased the team's rights to advertise on, around, and inside the stadium for an additional $60 million. And they christened it Invesco Field at Mile High.

But the fight in Denver was not over. The largest local paper, the *Denver Post,* refused at first to acknowledge the name. On August 8, 2001, Glenn Guzzo, the paper's managing editor, ran an editorial saying that the *Post* would never use the new name for the stadium. They would simply refer to it as "New Mile High Stadium." Guzzo wrote: "Excuse us. A noun *at* a compound adjective? Simply put, the proper response to this impossible name is: 'At Mile High what?' The community at large thinks of this as Mile High, New Mile High, or the new stadium. In this case, the community's terminology is familiar, positive, and clear." Guzzo noted in a later column that the stadium's name represented a moment in which it was more important to serve the public interest than a corporate one. The *Post*'s main competitor, the *Rocky Mountain News,* quickly accused the *Post* of a failure of journalistic integrity for not reporting the new name as fact.

Naming a sports stadium is an entrenched part of the modern sports-media-industrial complex. But in Denver, the tried-and-true recipe for brand growth backfired. Putting your name on a stadium seems to have jinxed companies in some weird cosmic way. Many of the firms that paid large sums of money to have their names listed on stadiums have seen incredible descents in stock values or were slowly going out of business. In 1999, Ken Lay, CEO of Enron, announced that the high-flying energy giant would pay roughly $100 million over thirty years to put its name on the new home of the Houston Astros. In January 2002, Enron filed for Chapter 11 bankruptcy, and the stadium went without a corporate sponsor for the first half of the 2002 season, until Coca-Cola's Minute Maid stepped up in June.

In April 2002, the old Mile High was demolished and replaced with 1,800 parking spaces. In June, the *Denver Post* hired a new editor, who reversed the decision to refer to the stadium as New Mile High. "We should call things what they're formally known as," he said, and from then on the paper used the stadium's new corporate name. In August of that year, the city renamed the street around the new stadium Mile High Stadium Circle—one more attempt to keep the name alive, to give something back to the public. In July of 2003, John Hickenlooper was sworn in as Denver's forty-third mayor after a landslide election and a campaign platform that portrayed him as the people's mayor and a "coalition builder who led the fight to keep the 'Mile High Stadium' name."

Those in charge of naming rights at the new stadium neglected a fundamental fact—that "Mile High" was an idea, not just a name. Attached to the idea of a stadium, it held a special meaning for the people of Denver, and that meaning was not so easily erased. "Mile High" was an idea that connected people to their city and gave them a sense of place. "Invesco Field" was not a logical substitute for what came before. Invesco is not the kind of word people would naturally copy and pass along—it is, at best, a truncation of *investment company,* a word distilled down to sound like a Southerner *drawing* it out. It is sterile, too, and a hard thing to sub in for Mile High.

For me, the Mile High conflagration was a way to get far away from the sterile whiteboards where most names are born and experience the passions ignited by naming, to leave the language lab and venture into the verbal wilderness. On the flight back home I thought about people fighting against commercialization. Some rail against brand names because they feel powerless in the face of them; others see them as oppressive forces moving commerce onto center stage worldwide and controlling minds all over. Naomi Klein, author of *No Logo: Taking Aim at the Brand Bullies,* is perhaps the most articulate brand detractor. Around the year 2000, as the idea of corporate branding became fully entrenched, Klein used her book to argue against the power of brands and to examine the dark side of this widespread and growing corporate orthodoxy. She writes of "the mounting stakes of brand-name protection" and shows how brands have invaded all spheres of public life and galvanized a large audience of protesters in a backlash against major brands. Klein's exhaustive documentation portrays large multinational corporate interests as consumer manipulators, using brands that entwine media and commerce to control the public. Some compared *No Logo* with Vance Packard's 1957 classic *The Hidden Persuaders. The Economist* called her book "a bible of the anti-globalization movement," which ensured that it would become required reading for brand strategists who hope to understand how to appeal to people who do not want to be appealed to.

In a similar vein, in *Culture Jam,* Kalle Lasn, the founder of *Adbusters* magazine, declared an end to global brands through a process of jamming them—using the brand equity of brands to destroy them. Lasn's "Culture Jammer's Manifesto" reads in part: "We will take on the archetypical mind polluters and beat them at their own game. . . . On the rubble of the old culture, we will build a new one with a noncommercial heart and soul." Lasn's idea was that holding sit-ins to protest corporate encroachment no longer worked. Trashing an icon—like a Niketown store or a Starbucks coffee shop—would send a message much farther and much faster. While I had thought about the so-called culture jammers and pondered their manifesto, I imagined a more agitated activist crowd. But preppy John Hickenlooper *was* a culture jammer, too.

Are brand names good or bad? In and of themselves they are neither, but what corporations do with them—how they insinuate them into the public arena—can cause problems. Although many activists and consumers alike see the ubiquity of brand names as signifying the homogeneity of worldwide capitalist culture, what some call globalization, there is also a growing awareness that, because brand names represent the trust held by a brand, that trust can be broken. And brand names do not create consumerism by themselves. Some might say that bottom-up branding is more insidious than top-down, for top-down is at least overt. A name is helpful because it helps us identify certain things we want to buy, but it becomes less helpful when we simply are drawn to that name through a form of commercial brainwashing.

Over time, a non-user-friendly name will be grudgingly shuffled into the local lexicon (look at San Francisco's 3Com Park), but Invesco could have gained much more from its multimillion-dollar sponsorship by listening to locals and crafting a name they might actually like. The main lesson from Mile High is that it's best not to force language into being; it's better to communicate with, not at, people. Or, better yet, have people communicate for you, as with *Whassup!*

Both of the above examples, *Whassup!* and the new Mile High Stadium, were appeals to similar audiences—drinkers of relatively inexpensive American beer and football fans. Budweiser's owner has its own stadium sponsorship, but in this case the marketing teams took widely different approaches to getting their words out. Accenture and Invesco got out only what they put in, the dollars paid. In the bottom-up scenario, a name is chosen because of its link to an existing cultural trend or idea, and the new word spreads by adhering to this idea. Instead of having to educate a consumer base about a completely fabricated name, the bottom-up name rides on the popularity of ideas already out there by becoming a part of a product story, in the way *Whassup!* did. That *Accenture* means nothing to me is not just a matter of aesthetics—it also limits the natural dissemination of the word, it flies in the face of how words naturally propagate and are shared. *Accenture* is not an idea but a top-down word. *Invesco* was launched top-down, and *Mile High* was an idea that had to be taken away first.

STORIES

9

"We tell ourselves stories in order to live," writes journalist Joan Didion in her book *The White Album*. "We live entirely . . . by the ideas with which we have learned to freeze the shifting phantasmagoria which is our actual experience." Didion's observations are surprisingly relevant to the spread of corporate language in general, and corporate stories in particular. We tell ourselves stories to make sense of the world. And the stories that we tell often are created from cues that surround us—parts of the story.

Stanford business school professor Chip Heath conducts research in business and the social sciences, an area of study he calls "the marketplace of ideas." He looks at the way ideas compete for attention, and the way they are disseminated. Heath sees ideas and stories as memes, the biological analogy for pieces of data that travel in an evolutionary fashion. These ideas undergo variation (new ideas differ), selection (the best ideas are chosen), and retention (the chosen pieces survive). Heath believes that memes succeed in part because of "emotional selection," because they evoke an "emotional reaction that is shared." In other words, people embrace ideas that provoke consistent emotional reactions. When Heath began to look at how ideas travel, the spread of urban legends that often take advantage of spurious associations provided a ripe area of study.

An urban legend is a fictional but true-sounding story told and retold in modern societies. Heath was attracted to urban legends because each one has some component that makes people want to share it with someone else. He was aware that many false "truths" percolate through communities. For example: that humans use only 10 percent of their brains, or that there are two hundred words for snow in the Eskimo vocabulary, how 70 percent of meals are eaten in automobiles, that 95 percent of running shoes will never be used for running, that 98 percent of SUVs will never be driven off-road, and that the "Marlboro man" died of lung cancer. After an unfortunate experience at Starbucks, writer Ron Rosenbaum floated his own hilarious urban-legend-in-the-making when he hypothesized in print that Starbucks could affect the productivity of American workers by tweaking the caffeine levels of its coffee.

Prominent brand names tend to adhere to corporate-related urban legends because these names are most easily recalled in retelling. In one case, an urban legend depicted beverage maker Snapple as a supporter of the Ku Klux Klan. The story produced outrage, and anger propelled the story forward. In another longstanding rumor, Procter & Gamble is portrayed as a Satanic enterprise. Fueled by an emotion, like anger, one person is compelled to share the tall tale with another. Heath discovered that stories survive not because of their informational content but because of their emotional impact. The ideas that punch emotional buttons in their listeners tend to survive better.

The lesson for the business community that Heath extrapolated from his study of urban legends is that corporate information, like mission statements, should incorporate more than straight facts. "If you are trying to inspire people, if you are trying to create something that's going to propagate on its own, you had better think about the emotional impact of what you are talking about, as opposed to just getting the facts out there," Heath told me. "People don't get excited about increasing shareholder value." They get excited about things that touch them emotionally—life, death, love, happiness.

Legend and myth are abundant in the corporate world. One positive urban legend holds that Southwest Airlines is the most consistently profitable airline and has more job applicants than any other carrier. Strangely enough, people who fly Southwest are often fans of the company's business model, which uses a point-to-point instead of a hub-and-spoke plane routing system. And at Stanford's Graduate School of Business, Southwest's case studies are the most frequently requested for outside purchase. Many business leaders are also fans.

Enron was a prime example of a company that had a story to tell. After the Texas firm outgrew its mandate to be "the world's leading energy company," and before its sensational collapse, chief operating officer Jeff Skilling floated the tag line "We Make Markets." The story that Enron told the world was a bold, well-fashioned tale about a company leading others in new ways. The company crafted a self-portrait that the public liked, and during the economic boom of the late 1990s investors were even less concerned than usual about the real facts and numbers behind companies. People "flocked to the companies that told the best stories," noted economist Paul Krugman in a column about Enron's fantastic fall from grace.

As a namer, I was struck by the fact that journalism and brand strategy are really two sides of the same coin. They both involve observing culture: one generally comments on the culture; the other tries to take the observations and capitalize on them. For commercial language applications, the namer's job is to study a culture so that a client can leverage new knowledge. In this way, namers are reverse-linguists, and corporate storytellers are reverse-anthropologists. Both have a hand in creating new words that are often synthetic forms that try to find a voice in the cultural din. And in the same way that brand names parallel real words, corporate stories parallel real stories.

The work done by namers and other consultants who assist in launching new forms of language has many similarities to the work conducted by academics in the fields of anthropology. Crossover from academic anthropology into marketing applications, or what has been called applied quantitative research, is a growing field. There are important differences, of course. A traditional ethnographer studies a foreign culture to codify its language, to record its materials and tools, and to make sense of the modes of operation within the culture. A namer or language consultant, on the other hand, seeks to study a language and its surrounding culture to understand the nuances of the language so they can create new words that will resonate in a particular culture and geographic area.

To anthropologists, culture is the body of learned beliefs, traditions, and guides for behavior shared among members of any human society, or the characteristic practices of a certain group of people. Human evolution is thought to have crossed a divide when culture superseded the environment as the major force in shaping the minds of people who lived as a social group. Once people no longer formed hunter-gatherer societies that migrated to follow food supplies, rooted agricultural communities took shape and spawned culture. With culture as the dominant force, the human being was no longer a natural inhabitant of the planet but a *product* of culture.

The founder of a company called Archetype Discoveries World-wide, Dr. G. Clotaire Rapaille works as a consultant to companies that span a number of industries, but mainly they sell automobiles. Rapaille is a good example of an anthropologist who works in the corporate world. Beginning in the 1970s, he consulted for Renault and Citroën in France before moving to the United States. In the mid-1990s, he worked at Chrysler with David Bostwick, Chrysler's head of market research, initially to determine why consumers were not buying many Chrysler cars. He helped Chrysler draw on consumer preferences to design the well-received PT Cruiser. Rapaille's work largely has been about identifying consumer sentiment and catering to it. One reviewer even called the PT Cruiser a focus group on wheels. Commenting on the success of the car, Bostwick said, "We didn't set out to create a market, we just tapped into what people had in their heads in the first place."

Rapaille saw the success of SUVs as a result of a dearth of cars that had a "face," some recognizable characteristic that made one car distinct from another. The PT Cruiser has a very recognizable face, he says. "People said 'I've seen this car' when we gave them a PT Cruiser." Rapaille told me that whenever you can polarize customers beyond a spectrum of likes and dislikes, you have a solid lock on the customer psyche, and a good product. Cars are no less important to people's self-identity than other products. "People wear a car like you wear a shoe," Rapaille told me.

Rapaille runs discovery sessions to formulate his theories on consumer behavior. His main technique, he says, is not to believe what people tell him in a direct focus-group-like setting. He prefers to circumvent the standard question-and-answer format of most focus groups where participants rarely provide true or helpful answers. He instead seeks to gather stories about first imprints—whether with cars, coffee, or hairspray—through "discovery sessions" that he sees as the antithesis of traditional focus groups. He wants to identify the emotional identity that the product holds for people based on their earliest encounter with it.

Rapaille strives to isolate the stories people have about certain experiences that have been imprinted in their minds. When he asks people about a certain subject—say, coffee—they tell him stories about the first time they smelled it brewing, or how their parents drank instant coffee, or the time when hot coffee spilled on their hand as a child. By looking at earliest encounters with products, listening to the words people recall, he attempts to discover the emotional identity that product holds for people. From an aggregate of the stories people tell him, he can identify a structure he considers pre-organized by society, by culture. In the case of coffee, imprints in people's minds led Rapaille to conclude that aroma was the unifying structure. We all have the word *coffee* imprinted in our minds; to launch a new company that would exist beside *coffee* or even replace it, Rapaille would seek to understand the cultural context of the term *coffee*.

Strong cultures, whether in or out of the corporate world, are often those with the best stories to tell. Culture, inasmuch as it influences the people who live under its sway, also has an impact on those who work in corporate environments, which we now call "corporate cultures." The notion of *corporate culture* was first discussed in the 1970s, when it began to appear on the periphery of business literature. Corporate culture, or *organizational culture,* as Harvard Business School professors John Kotter and James Heskett term it, has two parts. One level includes the values shared by people in a group; the other level is the behavior patterns or "style" found in an organization that new employees are encouraged to follow.

When a corporation launches a story into the world, or within the confines of its own organization, it does so with a goal of shaping behavior—similar to the goal a namer has. The story then spreads as a coherent way of thinking and has the potential to launch a whole way of thinking, to assimilate isolated ideas.

Disseminating a story is, by definition, a bottom-up and organic approach that creates something that has legs to travel on. A top-down approach is to fill up every available space so people will hear or see a name. Sometimes a brand name builds a story around it; at other times launching a story is the best way to get a brand name out into people's minds. Sending out a story that people themselves can tell can spread exponentially. With enough resources, a company can build a story and use its brand names in the story. The story itself should travel as a way of thinking.

IBM needed a new message to tell its customers, but before rolling out its traditional, top-down marketing campaign, the company sought to change its own culture by broadcasting a new story about itself. At IBM, the novel-like story it told in the mid-1990s was titled *e-business*. In the end IBM would spend more than $5 *billion* on an extended marketing campaign to promote that one little word.

FUTURECASTING

10

Working as a naming consultant and journalist in San Francisco, every so often I heard mention of a small firm called Stone Yamashita Partners. In hushed tones of reverence, fragments of the story emerged: that they worked for years with just one or two clients; that the firm was predicated on having a small, elite, very smart team; that clients trusted the firm to perform well and do the work of a much larger company; that co-founder Keith Yamashita advised more than one major CEO on leadership issues; that this group had created the term *e-business* for longtime client IBM.

Not given to self-promotion and happy to allow satisfied clients to pass along the good word, Stone Yamashita was a firm flying under the radar. I *googled* it but came up empty-handed. Its Web site featured statements that seemed obvious but at the same time unique and provocative: "Whoever controls the language controls the debate." But I still did not really understand what this group delivered to its clients.

A friend who had interviewed for a job with Stone Yamashita was my sole link. He told me that the consultants work at high levels of large companies to assist in defining important but vague issues like leadership, strategy, and vision. He said he had heard about a special book they wrote, a sort of summary of their philosophy—but he had not seen it.

When I finally called on Keith Yamashita, I acknowledged that I was intrigued by his company but unsure what exactly it did. A bit ambiguously, he replied, "We reinvent companies and we re-invent cultures." From the beginning, the firm was dedicated to helping clients launch ideas into the world, Yamashita explained. Now they were involved in launching full-fledged corporate cultures. And at the heart of any culture launch, according to Yamashita, is a story.

Stone Yamashita, I would eventually come to understand, was a team that found or made up stories and helped to tell them. The mission was to find the essence of a business or corporation, crystallize it, and then communicate it on two fronts: to employees so they know their role, and also to the outside world. The squad descended on behemoths like IBM and helped to galvanize the internal masses through rousing rhetoric. But telling stories? It sounded too simple—surely a large, successful company is more than a story well told. "There is no shortage of business strategies," Yamashita says. "Storytelling is about telling factual and strategic stuff in human ways so people will be moved. With great stories it becomes clear what you, the worker, are supposed to do."

That Stone Yamashita existed solely to help other companies tell their stories seemed to signal a dynamic shift in the corporate landscape. But it was all in the telling—not just the creation of the story but how the story was conveyed. The people at Stone Yamashita are a handpicked group trained to understand, decipher, and sometimes modify corporate cultures and then articulate the underlying story. Some consultants create names, some create ideas. A few, like Stone Yamashita, launch entire vocabularies. They systematize the language that serves as a foundation for corporate stories, and then they put the language to use, pouring it into corporate annual reports, executive speeches, and employee handbooks.

A name, an idea, and a corporate culture are all variations of a story. A name is the shortest, most distilled form of a story (like *BlackBerry*). An idea is the story behind a name, the associations that form a brand (like FedEx and "overnight"). Sprawling in a multitude of directions, a corporate culture is a further expansion, a novel-like story. If the story is good it can travel like a well-crafted name, with even more power to sway minds along the way. A culture has the ability to spread together as a whole way of thinking.

Creative Roots

Stone Yamashita is not easy to pin down. It is not an advertising agency, it is not a public relations firm, it is not a management consulting company, it is not a culture-change corps, and it is not a branding and design shop. In a lot of ways the Stone Yamashita team rolls these duties all into one. "The people at Stone Yamashita don't just craft strategy, they bring it to life," says Debra Dunn, vice president of corporate affairs for Hewlett-Packard, for which Stone Yamashita has worked since 1998. "Not only do they produce tangible outputs, but the experience of having a meeting or an engagement with them actually changes the way you approach your work." The group derives its mission from the ideas of cofounder Keith Yamashita, who is largely the face and the mouth of the company.

Although Yamashita, thirty-seven, talks in quiet, measured tones, a certain level of excitement is evident in his voice, and he laughs frequently when he makes a point. He is funny, youthful, smiles a lot, dresses casually in expensive clothes, and wears his thick black hair at shoulder length. He grew up in Orange County and went to college at Stanford, where he majored in quantitative economics. There he gained a solid understanding of the modern marketplace. He chose economics because he felt slightly guilty for the privilege of being at Stanford and wanted to take the most employable track. In the process of getting a master's degree in organizational behavior, he went on to study dysfunctional organizations, also at Stanford. He studied the question "How do you get teams to wrestle with ideas so that they can take action on them and make them their own?"

In 1988, Yamashita landed a job at Apple Computer as a senior writer in Apple Creative Services—the division responsible for strategic communications. There he met designer Robert Stone, an independent graphic designer brought in to work on packaging for Apple products. Yamashita served as creative director in charge of several brand launches at Apple, where he solidified an understanding and appreciation of the importance of language and its mostly overlooked role in business. Apple used language to great effect to position the company in a new place in the technology industry, and Yamashita had a hand in writing Apple's prolific prose.

He went from Apple to help at Steve Jobs's new venture, NeXT, where his duties included writing speeches, preparing brochures, and putting together videotapes for Jobs. NeXT was a vaguely defined company with a declared mission of supplying computers for higher education. In 1990, Apple brought Yamashita back to serve as creative director for the launch of Apple's first new brand in a decade—the Newton personal digital assistant. Yamashita, the youngest creative director in Apple's history (he was then twenty-four), led a team of thirty designers and writers. The Newton failed to take off (many thought it was ahead of the market; the Palm Pilot, introduced in 1996, eventually did what the Newton had been meant to do), and Yamashita moved on to write for Hal Riney & Partners, a large San Francisco advertising agency, where he found himself working on the launch of an entirely new car company—Saturn, a spin-off of General Motors. GM managers had decided that there was no way to launch a new compact car line within the culture at GM. There was a recognition that GM culture would hold back the new entrepreneurial project, so they spun it off as a separate company. A new message about the car spread because of this ultimately wise move.

At Hal Riney, Yamashita and his colleagues did a lot of the research into what would become the Saturn brand and decided to tell the tale in a way that was less sales-oriented ("Try Pepsodent!") and would speak more directly to people. "It was about pulling truth out of a culture, and having the culture connect with the truth," says Yamashita.

Presenting this truth involved a Saturn ad campaign that differentiated itself from all other car campaigns by telling a totally new story about the cars and the company that made them. The Saturn campaign had a human voice that told customers about the people who made the cars and the people who bought them. One early ad had an employee voice-over: "No one would ever ask me what I thought. Then I heard about Saturn building a whole new car plant to build a new car. And they figured out a new way of running things, too." At one point, more than 44,000 Saturn owners headed to Spring Hill, Tennessee, to participate in a gathering of customers called Saturn Homecoming. Owners barbecued, danced, and toured the car plant in a weird corporate fest that seemed to have been dreamed up by a postmodern fiction writer.

For Yamashita, Saturn was a pure example of the birth and

dissemination of a story that resonated with and attracted customers. Customers who bought Saturn cars left the car lot with Polaroid pictures taken with their salespeople—artifacts intended to disseminate a new message. Riney & Partners wrote owner manuals, developed the company's external communications, and produced internal culture videos. Saturn, the message, was primarily about how great the experience of buying and owning the car would be. It was, for Yamashita, an eye-opening look into "magnifying the truth within a culture."

All of Yamashita's experiences before he co-founded Stone Yamashita Partners with designer Robert Stone in April 1994 informed him of a shift in the marketplace: that companies were being forced to articulate their messages and their stories carefully to internal and external audiences. As more and more companies faced stiff competition in the 1980s, they squeezed every inefficiency out of production. But after doing so, they were unable to make comparable shifts in pricing and manufacturing techniques—traditional ways to face down competition. To boost sales, many turned to their brand images as a way to differentiate themselves.

In Yamashita's view, this was an easy way to go, to build value into intangibles—but it was a questionable tactic because it often failed to deal in depth with real, systemic change. There was more to it. Some companies even took to calling their brands stories—but to Yamashita, brands were just a part of the story: "Strong brand strategy is essential but not sufficient. We try to do more, to get to the root of the success." Most naming and branding is just an outer manifestation of the deeper issues, he says. In the Stone Yamashita model, a name is not enough—you have to create a whole way of thinking that remains coherent and disseminates as a unified concept.

Small Organizations

Stone Yamashita's offices are in a clean postindustrial loft building in San Francisco's South of Market neighborhood. The firm subscribes to an "open, chaotic, swarming method of doing work," according to Yamashita. Keeping everyone in one main parlor resembling a newsroom is crucial for collaboration. When you are weaving facts, information, and insights together for a client, the unofficial meetings are just as crucial as the official ones.

The average age of the workers at Stone Yamashita is around thirty-five, with a few twentysomethings on staff. Allison Koch, a member of the strategy team, calls it "work nirvana": an environment that fosters learning from inside and outside the company, interaction with amazing clients and leaders, and constant challenges. She also points to the great benefits, flexible scheduling and work hours, and competitive compensation. The number of staff is kept deliberately under thirty because the feeling is that the culture would inevitably change with greater numbers, and a larger group might detract from the brain trust already established.

This idea has been noted by academics like Robin Dunbar, a professor of psychology at the University of Liverpool. "Sociologists have long recognized that businesses of less than two hundred individuals can operate through the free flow of information among the members," writes Dunbar. "But once their size exceeds this figure, some kind of hierarchical structure or line management system is necessary to prevent total chaos resulting from failure of communication. Imposing structures of this kind has its costs: information can only flow along certain channels because only certain individuals contact each other regularly."

Unlike the employees of a traditional consulting firm like Accenture, Stone Yamashita's thirty employees must be versatile.

There is a recognition that when, in larger organizations, information does flow along traditional channels, things get lost in translation. In the same way that Lexicon prepares a word before it launches—ensuring that it is pronounceable and memorable—Stone Yamashita seeks to do this for an entire story. Because they know "information can only flow along certain channels" in larger organizations, their goal is to prepare a story for their clients that will transform these limited channels as it moves through them. Its own squad provides a laboratory for testing out communication ideas. Formally, the firm is split into three divisions—a writing team, a strategy team, and a graphic design team. Informally, the group includes an eclectic combination of professionals: a poet, a former journalist, a sociologist, a onetime telecommunications expert, and two ex-attorneys.

Historically, Stone Yamashita has had a main anchor client, like IBM, for whom it has worked for long periods on retainer. The firm also usually has a couple of shorter-term clients, which have included PwC Consulting, the Public Broadcasting System, Mercedes-Benz North America, Disney, AOL, idealab!, Kodak, and Microsoft. Generally, three client engagements are under way at any given time, with one principal from Stone Yamashita leading each project.

The notion of telling stories is vital to Stone Yamashita's operation, and it is far from limited to the verbal and linguistic sphere; graphic designers on staff are equally talented in presenting visual concepts. While the documents given to clients may have information similar to that provided by straight-shooting consulting firms like McKinsey and Bain, Stone Yamashita strives to make its documents more interesting to read, with interactive content and visuals so that clients can find their own part in the story, to engage.

During an ongoing engagement for the Public Broadcasting

System, Stone Yamashita put on several "experiential" summit meetings. They plastered meeting rooms with oversize posters featuring bold declarations that attracted participants' attention and encouraged them to interact so they might get involved in telling the story. After the meetings, they published a book that summarized everyone's ideas. Others might reduce the problems faced by a firm to a set of bullet points; Stone Yamashita wants to bring a less formal, less conservative, and more refreshing, candid tone to the work at hand. They are very focused on how to present information effectively.

As they note in *Seismic Change,* an in-house publication: "How you tell the story determines who will listen." This is another in-house mantra that applies in many ways. "PowerPoint is a lousy way to convey vision—because when you launch PowerPoint you immediately begin to think of expressing your thoughts only in bullet points, pie charts, and graphs. What makes a vision believable is the storyteller who paints a picture of what is possible. Consider dramatizing your vision in a different way—create a fable, a drama, an example. Fill a room with storyboards, fill the walls, make the story visual, compelling, worth hearing. Your audience will listen. Better yet, they'll engage. And that's the way you win converts. Get them to dive in on their own terms, and make the story their own."

Visions of e-business

IBM has a long, storied past. But the arrival of Stone Yamashita signaled a new period in which that story would succeed by getting broken apart, catalogued, examined, and retold. In 1995, when Robert Stone and Keith Yamashita got their first call from IBM, they claim to have been initially skeptical. It did not seem like an ideal project engagement for their nascent partnership.

Sitting in their offices in San Francisco, they could almost feel the *thump, thump, thump* as the commercial Internet was sputtering to life inside dozens of startup companies in adjacent buildings. Some were even clients. Nobody quite knew what the new medium was all about. Most of the initial uses of the World Wide Web focused on content—words, online publications, multimedia. Changes were happening every day. The Internet, they felt, was coming to San Francisco, not Armonk, New York, where IBM—that dinosaur of computing—was headquartered. This disconnect that they felt—between content and commerce—would become a pivotal insight in their work with IBM.

Stone Yamashita Partners went on to consult for IBM for more than four years. And the better they became at writing and articulating the IBM story, the more the company came to rely on them. They would codify the storytelling process as never before. IBM's founder, Thomas Watson Sr., had famously declared that "good design is good business." In a lot of ways, Stone and Yamashita were simply the newest team in a long line of creatives who had helped IBM over the years, including Charles and Ray Eames and Paul Rand, who designed the modern IBM logo.

Persuaded by their old Apple colleague Allison Johnson (who worked at IBM), Stone and Yamashita finally got on a plane in 1995 bound for the East Coast. They first worked on IBM's OS/2, then Johnson started working with a small new group at IBM: the Internet Division, charged with promoting a network strategy across all of IBM's business units. A major premise of the division was that the future of the Internet was really in online commerce, an area in which IBM had a lot to offer. Surfing the World Wide Web for content, they believed, would be secondary. The group needed help in clarifying its mission and communicating its role to the rest of the company. Johnson also sensed that the Internet would have some future impact on IBM at large.

The glimmerings of a vision were there, of a not-too-distant world where all companies conducted business on the Internet, and business became e-business. In this vision, IBM was the catalyst of change. It would bring companies from the offline world into the online one. IBM's technology would support the infrastructure necessary to build online businesses. Even more important, IBM's Services and Solutions Divisions would facilitate this step into the future. The team developed the idea that IBM's core asset was consistently being able to help other companies implement the technology that IBM created. This would be the big idea, the one they would run with: IBM provided solutions. IBM helped companies solve problems. IBM had already started using a slogan: "Solutions for a Small Planet." The company would make sure people understood IBM was going to help them do business online. And the heading under which the new story would be told was *e-business*.

As a word and an idea, *e-business* was already around the company and the industry when Stone Yamashita showed up. It had been used in correspondence at IBM, but nobody had done anything with it. Nobody yet owned the *story* of e-business, which is to say that nobody knew the story of how the Internet would play out in their line of products and services. IBM had to sort out that vision of the future. Stone Yamashita would help IBM "own" the idea—and own the story of e-business. Actual ownership of the word was not a priority as it was with, say, OS/2, ThinkPad, and System 360. Ownership of the *story* was critical.

In a lot of ways, the choice of the term *e-business* (over such other options as "network computing" and "Internet solutions") was not as difficult as the narrative that would flow from it, the text that would surround and promote the notion of e-business. To stake out new territory meant knowing that territory and IBM's role in it. At its best, Stone Yamashita helps its clients not by creating a simple, catchy, ownable word but by figuring out the larger picture, the industry-wide dialogue that the client should lead, and by creating all of the pieces that will make this possible. The approach was quite the opposite of the creation of an umbrella name, like *Accenture,* in which a new word would subsume all else. *Accenture,* as a corporate name, was a word that had to be owned above all else. *Accenture* was the big umbrella the corporation's words fell under. But to get *e-business* out there meant bringing everything else in line. Accenture had changed its role in its industry. IBM wanted to change the industry or, short of that, to ride the industry as it changed.

Owning the Story

To own the story, every single division at IBM had to get on board. "Formerly, naming was about control," says Yamashita. "Now you have to use nomenclature to latch on to ideas that are contemporary. You have to try to protect the core ideas in the story." This is done by first uncovering a company story and then evaluating its most valuable parts. The idea is to craft a message intrinsically interesting enough that people naturally want to pick it up. As it happens, almost a decade after the campaign was launched, that free word, *e-business,* remains favorably associated with IBM. The idea behind *e-business* was to recognize where the world was going—into an Internet-centric next stage—and to announce a name, an idea, and in the end a story, of which IBM (by being the first to talk about it) would be the owner. This marks a new way of thinking, especially for a large corporation. If you are going to be so bold as to send a new word into the data streams of the world, it has to be somewhat prophetic in what it says.

Although the prefix *e-* soon would become a ubiquitous part of the venture-capital-funded *e-* and *i-*everything Internet boom, in the early days it was new and different. It even managed to hold strong through the boom and bust of the Internet. To Stone

Yamashita, *e-business* was a *transitive* brand (a newer brand component that was separate from the main IBM brand, but if successful could become a part of the IBM brand). Because the general IBM brand had been tarnished by the financial turmoil the company had been through when it shrank from 430,000 employees in 1984 to 230,000 in 1993, and when revenues flattened in the late 1980s as IBM reported its first revenue losses since its founding in 1911, the company needed to rebuild credibility. As a transitive brand, *e-business* could be built with very little risk, and when it succeeded, the positive reception it received could be transferred back to the IBM brand.

Indeed, *e-business* as a meme, a piece of language that spreads on its own, served to shape the marketplace. At first competitors tried to avoid saying the word because they thought they would sound like they *were* IBM. At the same time they all wanted to be a part of e-business, and soon they came around as followers. Rival Oracle eventually launched its own E-Business Suite. At the end of 1996 and 1997, Stone Yamashita helped write IBM's annual report, telling IBM's story to the world. The 1997 report, subtitled *The New Blue,* said: "As a rule, we don't like to inject jargon into the language of information technology. But in 1997 we indulged ourselves. We coined the phrase 'e-business' to talk about the value our customers derive from networked computing. We also found that e-business is a powerful unifying message for IBM itself." (It was a bit of a stretch, though, as IBM did not really *coin* the term. But they certainly took ownership of it, and that was the original goal.)

Stone Yamashita and the IBM communications team worked with the leaders of various divisions to align all products with the vision. To mesh the internal strategy across the company, they made sure that *e-business* infiltrated every part: IBM Research, Global Services, the Software Group, and the Hardware Division.

"When we were working in the IBM Labs, we helped them talk

about what they do," recalls Stone Yamashita writer Maulhardt. " 'How is that related to e-business?' we asked. We asked them about their projects. They would say, 'I don't really have to think about things that way,' and we would say, 'If you want to make sure this project sticks around, it's probably a good idea to think about it that way.' So we ended up being the people who wrote much of the Internet Division's materials, but we also made sure that other divisions were writing materials that were at least considering this bigger strategy of e-business."

Lou Gerstner, the CEO of IBM since 1993, saw that *e-business* was a term that had to be infused with meaning so others in the industry would use it. "We had to strike a balance," he notes. "We wanted to be seen as the architects of e-business, the agenda setter for this new era, but we decided not to trademark the term 'e-business.' We couldn't make it an exclusive IBM term or idea. It was more important to build an awareness and an understanding around our point of view. Creating that environment would require massive investments, both financial and intellectual." The push was not so different from Anheuser-Busch's *Whassup!* media campaign, which spread virally with little in the way of legal ownership protecting it. And like Anheuser-Busch, IBM also would incur a high advertising bill.

Early in his tenure, Gerstner and his marketing head, Abby Kohnstamm, rounded up all of IBM's disparate advertising agencies—there were seventy all around the world—and fired every single one. In the biggest advertising-account shift in history, Gerstner sent IBM's multimillion-dollar advertising budget to one agency, Ogilvy & Mather, which in turn hired Steve Hayden— a dyed-in-the-wool former Apple advertising copywriter.

Hayden was in full agreement that *e-business* did not have to be owned by IBM—he knew the critical part was getting the story out fast and owning it. "We said, 'Open-source the name,' " recalls Hayden. (IBM was also the first large software writer to get behind open-source software like Linux.) It's a great example of the organic percolation of corporate language: When people have a hand in something and don't feel controlled, they often become greater proponents of that new idea.

Hayden saw no sense in controlling the word *e-business*. "We said, look, what you want to do is recognize where the world is going and announce it at just about the time when it occurs to everybody that it's arrived." He remembers telling IBM, "As a term it will decrease in value over time, but the world is moving so fast, there's no equity in hanging on to anything." Hayden says his team took the view that IBM did not really own anything anyway. "Because if nobody uses it—if the term isn't picked up, if it doesn't get into the language—then it has no value." IBM's new advertising agency would take the story to the outside world.

Hayden's most famous work with Apple had been co-writing Apple's Super Bowl commercial in 1984. Titled "1984," the ad showed an athletic young woman pitching a sledgehammer at a large, looming black computer—which many interpreted to be a frontal attack on IBM. *Advertising Age* would, in 1996, call this television ad the "greatest commercial ever." The spot, directed by *Blade Runner* director Ridley Scott, also transformed the Super Bowl telecast, taking television ad launches to a new level. Ironically, perhaps, Hayden came to serve as a vice chair at Ogilvy and chief steward of the IBM brand, a move he jokingly termed "the flip side of the coin, the dark side of the moon, the opposite equation."

By the time Hayden came to work for Ogilvy, he had joined the ranks of the ex-Apple mafia, a John Sculley–driven diaspora, people who left Apple looking for new creative challenges. Most of the people who understood the Apple brand fled the company during that mid-1990s low period. To Hayden it was a case of a company not valuing what people did, so they moved on. "You were left with kind of a bunch of old-school, golf-playing, beer-drinking, waitress-pinching computer salesmen," he said. There was no room for the language-obsessed, brand-attuned loyalists personified by co-founder Steve Jobs.

But Apple's training had provided them with an understanding of the value of a brand—even over a rational argument. "Literal-minded people will say things like 'the Mac advantage,' you know. And then Steve Jobs comes back and says, 'think different,'" says Hayden.

"Apple taught people the power of the irrational, and the importance of cool design," says Hayden. When someone buys an Apple, there's a good chance he or she is buying the brand first and the technology second. IBM, on the other hand, had strong technology but, as Hayden saw it, had to prove its humanity—while "understanding that people who read about technology are still people, and need to relate to a brand in an emotional way."

To take the message outside the company, Ogilvy created a three-phase advertising campaign. Most of the advertising material included an identifying mark, like Nike's swoosh. The "at-e" sign was similar to an @ sign (which had emerged as an icon of the Internet-oriented era), but with an *e* inside the circle. Using and asserting ownership of the special punctuation that came from the language itself—the @ sign—helped IBM own more of the e-business language. In phase one of the ad campaign, Ogilvy defined *e-business* in ways that were favorable to IBM. They educated their target audience about technology infrastructure and provided proof of IBM's expertise. In this way IBM began to "own" the e-business story. In the second stage, Ogilvy evangelized, telling companies just how they could become e-businesses with IBM's help. They gave examples of successful online businesses and showed the IBM technology that made success possible. Phase three, called "e-cultures" internally, was a worldwide poster series in which Ogilvy ran case histories of e-businesses— examples of Harley-Davidson, Yamaha, Vespa, Motorola, and others going online. The three messages, says Hayden, were "Here's what it is," "It's going to happen," and "It's happening." The underlying call to action shouted: *Don't let your company miss the boat.*

The advertising was high on "creative," a term that advertising writer Randall Rothenberg says stands for work that "kisses the irrational, emotional cheek of the human brain." Through the new advertising, too, the old image of an IBM worker—dressed in a blue suit and starched white shirt—came to be supplanted by an image of the new IBM worker sporting a black turtleneck. Apple's Steve Jobs, of course, was the original CEO-in-a-mock-turtleneck. The image of a more hip worker was not just for the outside world but also allowed IBM ranks to see themselves in a new light.

When Gerstner stepped in as CEO to aid the ailing IBM in 1993, he found a group of investment bankers mentally carving up the corporation into parts that could be sold off. To them the company was like a cow ready for slaughter, so Gerstner's first job was to rescue IBM from this fate. When someone asked him what his vision was, he famously answered, "The last thing IBM needs is a vision, right now." Many reporters cut the "right now" off his remarks, spreading a more severe message than Gerstner intended. It was a way of saying, "Let's not get paralyzed by outthinking our way out of here," recalls Yamashita. Years later, Gerstner would say that he was declaring a break with the old IBM culture of introspection—for him to have floated a "vision" would have led to widespread and long-term debate. He did have a vision, though, and it was that the company was going to move in response to the customers, to the marketplace.

In his first eighteen months, Gerstner concentrated on stabilizing IBM. He made a lot of difficult decisions, including job and infrastructure cuts necessary to keep the company together. By the time Stone Yamashita arrived, IBM was ready for Gerstner's customer-focused vision: e-business would be something for customers to talk about. At the time, Gerstner said, "e-business is not just sticking a Web site out there. It's not about Web browsers. It's about changing the whole way you do business inside the company and outside the company." Gerstner saw e-business as more than an integrating program for the company on a strategic and operational level; for him, it was a "galvanizing mission" that gave IBM "both a marketplace-based mission and a new ground for our own behaviors and operating practices—in other words, culture." Corporate storytelling would help customers develop their own narratives about getting into e-business.

One Voice

To take a message outside, first you have to share the message inside. The centerpiece of IBM's new e-business strategy was a sixty-six-page booklet that shipped out of IBM's global headquarters in Armonk, New York, titled *One Voice*. Postmarked February 1997, this booklet had been translated into six languages and was headed in 230,000 different directions—to the home addresses of every IBM employee around the globe. On page 2, seven white words on a black background read succinctly, "Telling the IBM story to the world." *One Voice* had the same goals as a quick retreat under the auspices of Stone Yamashita—to refocus the company's mission, and get all the employees on the same page.

Under a heading that read "The Revolution Will Touch Every Part of IBM," employees were encouraged to think about how a new era driven by network computing would affect their work: "You might be tempted to believe that someone else at IBM is doing the work, that your division and team can just keep on doing what you've always done." A couple of questions were posed: "How will your unit contribute to IBM's overall offering in network computing? How will *you*?"

At the end of the booklet, the ideas were summarized:

1. Network computing is reshaping our entire industry, and we're mobilizing every part of IBM to get behind this revolution.

2. But more than a business opportunity, this is a chance to regain leadership at the center of our industry.

3. Network computing plays to IBM's strengths. We have clear advantages, beginning with the breadth of resources and talents in our three core businesses: Solutions, Services, Products and Technologies.

4. To succeed, we are changing our corporate culture. We must move at warp speed, break down barriers between teams, and execute decisively.

5. Every single one of us is critical to pulling this off.

6. Think. And then do.

So what was *One Voice*? It was part corporate manifesto, part mission statement, part pep rally, part brand guideline, and part employee handbook. But if it was a mission statement, it was a lengthy, sprawling declaration—not really a *statement*. As a corporate manifesto it came close—but it was written in too much of a conversational tone. As an employee handbook it was far too contemplative. It was not a corporate myth, either. It was an outline of a story being told, a story about IBM. Properly executed, the story would first sway IBM's own workers and sweep them up in it—they would all become actors in and tellers of the story. The corporate culture would change. And then the story would sway the outside world, for IBM, like any company, cannot exist without customers.

As the story spread through the vast reaches of IBM, the company began to shift focus. The story captured people in its narrative, changing their views about the company they worked for and the industry in which that company operated. No major changes were made in the corporate organizational charts. Instead, this staple of IBM culture actually was tossed aside. And the product lines were not vastly altered, either. But a new narrative emerged with as much power as any of these changes might have had, and maybe even more. There was a new word to rally around— *e-business*—and the word was the title for the entire story. The goal was to own the story—and to tell it to the world.

Getting the story right was perhaps the most difficult step. To know the opening lines of the story meant knowing the last lines of the story. To create a compelling story, you had to work backward, from the end to the beginning—it was a feat of reverse engineering. Deciding on a vision—an end for the story, a goal to reach—was the first step. Then you had to communicate the vision through various channels inside and outside the company (epitomized by *One Voice*). The result, if all went as planned, would be an epic and highly rewarding culture change. A firm would move in a new direction, an army of 230,000 would swing into action, focused on a new goal.

One Voice was a bold move. It was a gamble that all the parts of the story, the chapters, would fall in line—which is why IBM turned to Stone Yamashita, whose members roved the corporate halls and learned the company inside and out, while slowly gaining the trust of the people who worked there. The outside team spent months deciphering IBM in the process of writing the new story. They came prepared—they had an outsider's vantage point that was essentially West Coast thinking in an East Coast company, and a working thesis that nailing down the IBM story would save the day. In their own words, they were a firm that combined energy with intellect.

Stone Yamashita had to figure out how much of their Apple training was appropriate for a company like IBM, a much more complicated place. The IBM way of speaking was a bit aggressive. They had to soften the tone a little bit—using the skills that they had learned from what Stone Yamashita writer Lisa Maulhardt calls "the happy and pleasant and human Apple voice."

At Apple, the concentration on language had long been an integral part of the company; all company communications were sharply watched by an editorial team. Any words headed for the outside world went through this filter before becoming Apple prose. In this way, the Apple story remained consistent.

Lisa Maulhardt, who was a writer at Apple, recalls that the editorial board at Apple "would mark up your work, and suddenly it would have a different flow so it would sound like Apple. We got used to taking their guidance, and then ultimately it became second nature to us." A lot of this perfectionist work ethic trickles down from founding CEO Steve Jobs, who famously hangs on—and bets everything on—every decision. The training at Apple was critical to shaping the Stone Yamashita sensibility, says Maulhardt. "It really helped us be super-attentive to language—and not only grammar, but pacing, simplicity, and directness, and figuring out how that translated into a personality for a company."

Stone Yamashita's thinkers emerged from Apple having gained an understanding of the importance of a corporate culture. Technology companies once were valued because their technical sophistication aimed at a very specific engineering audience. More recently they have come to realize that this was not enough. "Simplifying what they say has been something that all the big companies have done, and in simplifying they all start to sound the same," notes Maulhardt. The message, she says, is ultimately "We're going to make your life easier." This, of course, has been the Apple message all along. When it comes down to it, Hewlett-Packard, IBM, and other competitors are all selling servers, software, and services—essentially the same products. "Differentiation is a big deal, and sometimes the differentiation happens in the culture," says Maulhardt.

One Voice, as an outline of the story, was a key part of bringing the IBM masses into the story. "This was a vision strategy," says Yamashita. "Not just a pure statement of who you aspire to be— it gave a pragmatic pathway." *One Voice* had currency. After the initial run, another 500,000 copies were printed; then came a sequel—a much more technical document. Eventually it took on a life of its own. Salespeople gave it to customers. HR used it for recruiting. It became must-reading for managers. *One Voice* did not change IBM, but it reoriented its strategy and changed the culture.

People carried it with them and read it like a bible. Corporate communications head Jon Iwata remembers being on an IBM jet and noticing a senior executive pull out a dog-eared copy to study it. Other IBM executives called the document "corporate religion and corporate doctrine rolled into one."

Chemistry

To give me a better grasp on his firm, Yamashita sent me home with a weighty book that he and his staff had published recently. In clean red letters on the spine and on its cover, the book was titled *Chemistry: And the Catalysts for Seismic Change.* The book intentionally was made to look like an elementary school textbook, circa 1959. This was *the* book that I had heard about long ago, the one that had furthered my interest in Stone Yamashita.

While some firms might slave over a fancy brochure, this was a tome of more than five hundred pages, stitched together in leaves so that one had to literally cut pages apart to read the half of the book still trapped behind perforations. My interest was piqued by this self-published volume created by a discreet firm that worked exclusively with the top executive management teams of top-echelon firms in corporate America. The company itself had extended its talents to tell its own story. The book was filled with provocative charts and illustrations. There were plates reminiscent of a science textbook, and plenty of circular Venn diagrams showing the interrelations of various concepts. Finally I had my own copy. Back at my office, I sat down, slit open all the pages, and read the entire book.

Reading the firm's magnum opus, I wondered what drove the process of creating it. Then I realized that *Chemistry* was an exercise, too—an internal exercise driven by the same ideas that govern client engagements. Each Stone Yamashita player, whether a writer, a designer, or a strategist, engaged in the process of self-reflection and production that yielded *Chemistry*. It was a way for a cohesive team to codify its own story, to record it in one place. The IBM project had been a four-year journey, a testing ground for Stone Yamashita's ideas. Like any brochure that aims to sway its readers—to attract and retain clients—it is a sales tool. In *Chemistry* you see the Stone Yamashita master plan, its formula for success laid out in a systematic way.

Yamashita said *Chemistry* was a way for the firm to write down all the lessons it had learned in eight years of business. Among those lessons it interwove outside texts. A critic might allege that *Chemistry* and *Seismic Change* (a smaller brochure) were simply outlandish books that created their own vocabulary to state otherwise obvious things. At their worst, these documents resembled the point-of-sale business books that have bloomed over the last ten years—with names like *Kung Fu in the Boardroom* and *Fighting the Giant Rhinoceros*—filled with generic aphorisms but little substance. But Stone Yamashita's books had appealing design and demonstrated literacy and fluency with more than just basic business concepts, reaching far outside of the business world and away from the simple notions about "killing the competition."

Stone Yamashita created around 2,500 copies of *Chemistry* in July 2001 and gave them out slowly and selectively, mostly to current and past clients. It's clear from reading *Chemistry* that the IBM engagement was the proving ground for Stone Yamashita— and for Yamashita's profound belief in the power of storytelling. IBM was a place to test the Stone Yamashita master plan. If it could change a massive company like IBM, it was onto something. Having achieved success at IBM, the firm chose to write down the formula, rally behind it, and share it.

Reading *Chemistry* is a deep indoctrination into this worldview. In the Stone Yamashita construct, as laid out in *Chemistry,* there are five chief components at play in a corporation. Leadership is the glue holding the pieces together. A vision comes first, followed by communication of the vision, followed by culture change. Alterations in experience—for both consumers and employees—are the goal.

"Why work?"

In 1998, while Stone Yamashita was busy inculcating IBM divisions on the new e-business story, the firm began working with the human resources division on a college recruiting campaign. The goal was to identify a message that would mesh with IBM's overarching new story, and that IBM could use to attract new job candidates. This was a time when many talented students were heading off to venture-capital-backed startups and incubators. Stone Yamashita, in its usual self-reflective way, had already done much of the groundwork for this new undertaking: All through their project engagement, the team members had asked *them-*

selves what would make them want to work at IBM, to switch from consultants to full-tilt IBMers. This was a curiously honest approach to an age-old question faced by most consultants who work at client offices. The new project was a way for them to sum up what they thought was great about IBM. They took this thread of an idea and queried people all over the company. They whittled down their thoughts and their research to a simple question: Why work? "We both knew that IBM was better served by attracting people who were more interested in the question than in providing a pat answer," they later noted.

In the same way that *e-business* was a term surrounded by a story, "Why work?" was really a simple question that could be applied to any company, in any industry. "Why work?" asked people to think about a deep question. And, having posed that question, having created a forum for debate, IBM (as it would own *e-business* in the minds of so many) would also own this debate. "Why work?" was essential to attract new talent to work at IBM and to retain the best employees—a critical component of the new IBM story.

The recruiting campaign sought to match people's passions to the work at IBM. By asking "Why work?" recruiters were in effect asking prospective employees what their passions were, what they wanted their colleagues to be like. They wanted people to think about what made work important to them. In Yamashita's words, the campaign "played not to the lowest common denominator, but the highest shared common purpose."

Having learned what the culture was all about at IBM, Stone Yamashita was able to link the culture with the new strategy. As Lou Gerstner would say on his departure from the CEO's office in 2002, sounding as if he'd taken a page out of the Stone Yamashita book, "You can't talk a culture into changing. You can't just exhort people to be different. You've got to point to fundamental strategic changes you're going to implement in a company and then drive the execution of that strategy. And it is in the execution of the strategy that the culture begins to change."

In other words, you lay out the story—the strategic changes—and as people fall in line and execute the strategy, the culture follows. That is the essence of the Stone Yamashita formula. Instead of telling people what to do, you get those people to carry the torch, to tell the story in their own words. It's a bottom-up approach, almost a grassroots movement, that's pretty rare in corporate America.

So, in the end, had IBM told the IBM story "to the world"? You can see the new IBM story play out in the business press. In the early 1990s, business writers had taken IBM to task for losing its visionary status—but by 2002, it received accolades.

In their 1994 best-selling book *Built to Last,* Stanford business school professors James Collins and Jerry Porras thought about what they would say to IBM executives if they were called on. "We'd challenge them to set a BHAG [Big Hairy Audacious Goal]. . . . We'd challenge IBM to once again obsolete itself, to bet the company on the success or failure of that BHAG, just like it did on the System 360 [a new mainframe computer technology]. We'd challenge them to have faith that IBM people would come through and achieve the impossible again, just like they did on the 360. IBM has great people, and they would undoubtedly rise to the task." Porras and Collins explained that they would challenge executives at IBM to revisit what the authors call their "three basic beliefs." And they wrote that they would "challenge them to ask every employee in the company to personally rededicate himself or herself to the three basic beliefs." Unknown to Porras and Collins, at the time their book was being printed, IBM—under the supervision of CEO Gerstner and with the help of Stone Yamashita—was doing all of this.

Around 1997, perceptions began to shift. IBM's changes were noted by the outside world. Jean-Marie Dru, the French advertising executive and writer, noted that IBM had staged a spectacular recovery. "Every aspect of the company has been reassessed," noted Dru. "A lot has changed, and this transformation obviously had to be reflected in IBM's advertising. IBM now presents itself as the provider of 'solutions for a small planet.' IBM is recentering itself precisely on what made it successful, as a company that guarantees solutions. IBM has refocused its original vision."

By the time Scott Bedbury, the branding guru who led the Nike and Starbucks marketing departments sequentially in the 1990s, sat down to write his own book on branding in 2001, he saluted IBM. IBM had entered the realm of all-star brands Saturn, Nike, Coke, and Starbucks. He called IBM's execs "brand environmentalists," which in his view meant taking on a responsibility to protect one's brand and present it in the best possible light in all contexts.

The press, as it happened, took to the IBM story. A reporter for the *New York Times* had pronounced IBM irrelevant in 1992 in a front-page article titled "The IBM Era Is Over." He noted that the company no longer would set the pace of technological innovation, after having done so for decades: "One of the world's most vaunted high-tech companies has been reduced to the role of a follower, frequently responding slowly and ineffectively to the major technological forces reshaping the industry." Economist George Gilder was quoted, citing "the law of the microcosm" as an underlying reason for IBM's decline.

By 2002, the *Times* took a remarkably different angle: "The revival of IBM over the last nine years is most tellingly measured not in numbers but by its return to pre-eminence as the industry leader. Once again, IBM is the model others follow." The *Times* noted: "At the conclusion of Mr. Gerstner's tenure, his three strategic pillars have come together in what could be mistaken for the very word he avoided, a vision. And that strategy shift, actually executed, ensured a real change in the corporate culture."

With the help of Stone Yamashita, IBM managed to shape the industry-wide dialogue and take a leadership position in it. *e-business*. All had followed the story. As Lou Gerstner noted, the *e-business* campaign "helped establish IBM as the leader of the most important trend in the industry at that time." Indeed, the power of a strong, concise, and contained message is capable of swaying vast opinion and altering the opinions of a supposedly critical press corps, whose views may in the end be shaped by advertising and public relations messages in ways similar to members of the public. And with the press engaged, even more of the public can be engaged—refracting a message that helps refuel its own spread.

It's important to note that IBM used every possible communications channel at its disposal to get its message out. The goal would be to lead the industry, but to get there they had to start internally—*One Voice*—and move to attract and retain talent—"Why work?"—and then take the message to the masses—*e-business*. In essence, an integrated communications platform that swept up many—employees, customers, competitors, and the press—into a narrative, an IBM story.

IBM's people had told the story to the world. And the story had swayed the people.

SUMMING UP

11

I've stepped back in time, wound the clock a decade back, to 1994. Someone hands me a sheet of paper with five words typed out. BlackBerry. Accenture. Viagra. Cayenne. e-business. Each word means very little to me. *BlackBerry* is, of course, a fruit. Its innercapped *B* is strange, leading me to think of the word as a brand name like *AstroTurf*. *Accenture?* I have no idea what this word means. Someone has made it up. *Viagra* somehow seems more real, more tied in to the hundreds and thousands of words that have been organically birthed—not sketched on whiteboards. *Cayenne* is a spice. And *e-business,* if I am prophetic I can guess that this is some new direction business will take, into the electronic sphere. This word that seems untethered to any company is perhaps related to the embryonic World Wide Web.

Fast-forward to 2004. Each of these words has dozens of connotations for me. As a consumer I know each brand message, and after I've traveled from San Francisco to Germany to examine where these words came from, I have a whole new set of connotations based on the people I've met along the way.

Starting off on the journey that became this book, I did not know much about the variations among the contemporary crop of brand names. I knew instinctively that *BlackBerry* seemed like a unique and approachable name for a product that I might want to check out. I was less drawn to *Accenture*—a word that did not entirely repel me but seemed lifeless, synthetic, and ugly. *Viagra* seemed powerful, interesting, and tightly constructed. While Porsche itself represented a distinctive product, the Cayenne seemed a poor choice as an idea for a vehicle, and its name was far from the graceful and powerful group of words that Porsche had made its own. *e-business,* too, seemed uninspired and sounded generic.

Regardless of my opinions, this was a crop of successful words—each with something to teach. And it turned out that my gut reactions had a basis: I was more drawn to the words launched in a bottom-up fashion, set out there for me to discover instead of feeling controlled by them. *BlackBerry* proved to be a quintessentially bottom-up word, a niche-defining name to which people naturally gravitated. As a top-down name, *Accenture* took an opposite tack, a made-up word launched with an extensive advertisement-as-education technique. *Accenture* embraced its umbrella-like nature, and one had to gain familiarity with the word before appreciating it. *Viagra* was launched bottom-up, and people passed on the word and made an idea out of it. *Cayenne,* top-down and tied to Porsche—has a future that remains uncertain, but its creators studied their audience so as to better speak to them. IBM decided not to rely on words alone, but on a story that people would want to tell. *e-business* became an exemplary (if expensive) lesson in bottom-up naming and storytelling. And like *BlackBerry*, the word had been around—both successes relied on proper treatment of the words.

One of the more interesting aspects of reporting on the consulting firms in this book was that each had its own story to tell, stories that served as sales tools for clients and ways for employees to understand their roles. At Lexicon, the story is about a small firm content with doing one thing well—producing succinct strings of letters. At Wood Worldwide, the story is similar—but tied to the healthcare industry and the vicissitudes surrounding regulatory approval and rapidly changing consumer behavior. At Stone Yamashita Partners, it is a story about a cadre of master storytellers able to discern existing tales and create new narratives to inspire action.

People turn to brands for a number of reasons. For some, brands have become dependable replacements for a lost sense of societal values: *Gymboree* standing for wholesome, carefree children's play; *Volvo* representing safety; the local *Starbucks* substituting for the small-town diner. Brands can be shorthand for the things that people want to communicate about themselves. Some turn to brands because they stand for sets of ideas that they hope to possess. And brand names also can serve as tools to help people navigate through an increasingly complex world. Trusting a brand name is often easier than researching each purchase. It's a lot easier to remember the Sears *Weedwacker* than its competitors' *string trimmers* and *garden edgers*. The stories presented in this book all show the power of language to affect and change human behavior.

Sometimes these words have too much power over us. We have to stay aware. Are my senses dulled, is my vocabulary less rich, because of the many brand names I know? I have little doubt that our individual vocabularies are shrinking in parallel to the disappearance of the world's languages. Is it a problem that in my reduced yet brand-saturated vocabulary a larger proportion of words has something to do with buying and consuming? I think it is. Do I want to live in David Foster Wallace's "Year of the Depend Adult Undergarment"? I do not.

The best words will be like Maverick and his cows. For language to continue to shape and move behavior, even as the commercialized world gets noisier, attention to proper language will be of greater importance, and of greater worth to anyone launching words. Those who study and emulate the traditional, organic growth of new words—and the migration of words into the body of language—will find the greatest success by speaking clearly. The best words, like Maverick's cows, will continue to "graze, to fatten, to multiply, and to wander away."

NOTES

1. Hunting Words

page 3: "communication is no longer a product *attribute*," from Jean-Marie Dru, *Disruption: Overturning Conventions and Shaking Up the Marketplace* (New York: John Wiley & Sons, 1996), 213–14.

page 3: "the act of learning language," from Robin Dunbar, *Grooming, Gossip, and the Evolution of Language* (Cambridge: Harvard University Press, 1996), 3.

page 4: "are almost complete advertisements," from Claude Hopkins, *My Life in Advertising* (Lincolnwood, Illinois: NTC Business Books, 1987), 312.

page 5: "lingua branda," from Geoff Nunberg, "Farewell to the Alero," National Public Radio, *Fresh Air,* 14 February 2002.

page 5: "What is really being bought," from Jeremy Rifkin, *The Age of Access* (New York: Tarcher/Putnam, 2000), 47.

page 13: The experiences of Andrea Carla Michaels come from interviews I conducted with her. Additional reporting about Andrea also comes from a National Public Radio *All Things Considered* interview with Andrea conducted by Bob Garfield on 23 November 1995. Garfield's story served as background on Andrea's work as a namer and on her participation on *Wheel of Fortune*.

page 14: "Naming is like songwriting," from an interview with Andrew Chaikin, 24 October 2001.

2. Camouflage and Code Names

page 35: The first mention I saw of the Cayenne was in "Porsche May Add New Product After its Cayenne S.U.V.," Reuters, 7 December 2000.

page 35: Porsche's description of the name *Cayenne* is from "Hot Property: Top Secret—or How the New Porsche Sports Utility Vehicle Came By Its Name," *Christophorus,* August–September 2000.

page 36: Wendelin Wiedeking quote in Porsche press release dated 7 June 2000, http://www3.us.porsche.com/english/usa/news/pressreleases/-pag/000607.htm.

page 43: The Ford Correspondence from *A Marianne Moore Reader* (New York: Penguin, 1961), 215–24.

3. BlackBerry: Sending a Quick Message

The bulk of the information in this chapter came through interviews with David Placek, Marc Hershon, and Steve Price of Lexicon, and with Dave Werezak of Research In Motion.

page 51: "To Paul Taylor, Coca-Cola's director," quoted in Seth Stevenson, "I'd Like to Buy the World a Shelf-Stable Children's Lactic Drink," *The New York Times Magazine,* 10 March 2002.

page 52: "The key to the success," from Kevin Maney, "BlackBerry: The 'Heroin' of Mobile Computing," *USA Today,* 7 May 2001.

page 53: "treatment effects and selection effects," from Bruce Headlam, "Nothing Personal," *The New York Times Magazine,* 17 February 2002.

page 57: "It is the price of progress," from William Whyte, Jr., *The Organization Man* (New York: Simon & Schuster, 1956), 58.

page 57: "The term *groupthink,*" from John Schwartz and Matthew L. Wald, " 'Groupthink' Is 30 Years Old, And Still Going Strong," *New York Times,* 9 March 2003.

page 60: "the television, which spread from a 9 percent saturation," from Cobbett S. Steinberg, *TV Facts* (New York: Facts on File, 1980).

page 60: "the Engel Curve" from Mary Douglas and Baron Isherwood, *World of Goods: Towards an Anthropology of Consumption* (London: Routledge, 1996), 98.

page 61: "Institute for the Future," Pitney Bowes's *Workplace Communications in the 21st Century,* 1998.

page 65: "Consonants called 'obstruents,' " from Bob Cohen, "There's More to a Name," *Stanford Business School Magazine,* March 1995.

page 66: "The ultimate awareness," from David Aaker's *Building Strong Brands* (New York: Free Press, 1996), 15.

page 67: Description of the Swiffer licensing and marketing from Richard Curtis, "New Swiffer Cleans up for Procter," *Cincinnati Business Courier,* 5 November 1999.

page 73: United States Congress BlackBerry use, from Ephraim Schwartz, "Congress Bets on BlackBerry," *InfoWorld,* 12 October 2001.

page 73: Nokia's "Brick," from Paul de Bendern, "Nokia's 'brick' hand-held to hit shelves this summer," Reuters, 21 January 2002.

page 74: "Who wins between an alligator," quoted in Bill Breen, "Rapid Motion," *Fast Company,* August 2001.

4. Maverick Thinking

page 78: H. L. Mencken discusses the issue of Maverick's "stealthy branding" briefly, as well as the origin of some brand names and other words in a section titled "The Making of New Nouns," in his comprehensive book *The American Language: An Inquiry into the Development of English in the United States* (New York: Knopf, 1962), 189.

page 78: "into [the cows'] tender hides," from the writings of George Maverick and John Henry Brown that are included in *Mavericks: Authentic Account of the term "Maverick" as Applied to Unbranded Cattle,* © 1937 Rena Maverick Green.

page 81: "those who trumpet the power of the brand," from James Surowiecki, "The Billion-Dollar Blade," *The New Yorker,* 15 June 1998.

page 81: Sale of Kraft from David Aaker's *Managing Brand Equity* (New York: Free Press, 1991), 8.

5. Accenture Adapts to the Future

page 84: Much of the historic background on Arthur Andersen comes from Harvard Business School case: Professor Ashish Nanda, *Family Feud: Andersen versus Andersen (A and B),* 24 February 2000.

page 86: "Consulting became a goal for many graduating seniors," from Nicholas Lemann, "The Kids in the Conference Room," *The New Yorker,* 18 October 1999.

page 88: Andersen Consulting revenues from Accenture 2001 Annual Report. Figures are worldwide revenues (before reimbursements) in U.S. dollars for years ending August 31.

page 88: Some background on Andersen in the mid-1990s comes from Elizabeth MacDonald and Joseph B. White, "Generation Gap: At Arthur Andersen, the Accountants Face an Unlikely Adversary," *Wall Street Journal*, 23 April 1997.

page 89: "Reputation by Choice," presentation by George T. Shaheen, 9 November 1993, in court documents: *Andersen Consulting Business Unit Member Firms v. Arthur Andersen Business Unit Member Firms and Andersen Worldwide Société Coopérative*, 9797/CK/AER/ACS, The International Court of Arbitration International Chamber of Commerce, Geneva, Switzerland, 28 July 2000. Included in *American Review of International Arbitration* 10, no. 4 (1999). © Juris Publishing, Inc.

page 90: "a global divorce proceeding," from Barry R. Ostrager, Peter C. Thomas, and Robert H. Smith, "Andersen v. Andersen: The Claimant's Perspective," *American Review of International Arbitration* 10, no. 4 (1999): 443. © Juris Publishing, Inc.

page 90: "This is very significant," quoted in Deepa Babington, "USA: Accenture Now a Clear Winner Without Andersen Name," Reuters English News Service, 17 January 2002.

page 90: "He resigned four hours after," from Ken Brown, "Andersen Consulting Wins Independence—Arbitrator Tells Firm to Pay Auditing Arm $1 Billion; Parent's Role Criticized," *Wall Street Journal*, 8 August 2000.

page 95: "A memo went out from Jim Murphy," from *Accenture: The Rebranding and Repositioning Documentary*, 28 March 2001.

page 96: "will stretch, but not beyond," from Al Ries and Jack Trout, *Positioning: The Battle for Your Mind* (New York: McGraw-Hill, 2001), 123.

page 97: "Born in 1913 and raised," quoted in Stephen Bayley, "Obituary: Walter Landor, Herald of the Corporate Image," *The Guardian*, 16 June 1995.

page 97: "gathering of communicators," from Howard Gossage, Jeffrey A. Goodby, and Bruce B. Bendinger, eds., *The Book of Gossage: A Compilation Which Includes "Is There Any Hope for Advertising?"* (Chicago: Copy Workshop, 1995), 275.

page 97: "great package design flagship," from Tom Wolfe's *The Pump House Gang* (New York: Farrar, Straus & Giroux, 1968), 141.

page 98: "Of course," quoted in Wolfe, *The Pump House Gang*, 142.

page 99: "derived from the Latin *altus*," from Philip Morris advertisement, *New York Times*, 19 November 2001.

page 101: The birth of brands is described well in Naomi Klein's *No Logo: Taking Aim at the Brand Bullies* (New York: Picador USA, 1999), 6.

page 101: "A nationwide vocabulary," from J. Abbot Miller and Ellen Lupton, *Design Writing Research: Writing on Graphic Design* (New York: Kiosk, 1996), 177. This work also is cited in Klein, *No Logo*.

page 102: Charles Shaw wine from Frank J. Prial, "For $2, a Bottle of Wine and Change," *New York Times,* 23 April 2003.

page 103: On umbrella names, Julie Cottineau, director of naming at Interbrand, said in an interview on 8 August 2001: "A lot of the names that you see like Verizon, meaningless names, are created because of the trademark squeeze and also because of the fact that corporations have to have larger umbrellas to fit all of which they do underneath."

page 103: Agilent naming from Ruth Shalit, "The Name Game," *Salon.com,* 30 November 1999.

page 106: The thirty-plus candidates are shown in *Accenture: The Rebranding and Repositioning Documentary,* 28 March 2001.

page 110: "Andersen Consulting is a big success story," from Al Ries, *Focus: The Future of Your Company Depends on It* (New York: HarperBusiness, 1997), 230.

page 110: "wordmark would be at the center," from "The Rebranding Story," Accenture Web site, http://www.accenture.com/xd/xd.asp?it=enWeb&xd=aboutus\history\rebrand\over_rebrand_news.xml.

page 111: "Joe Forehand saluted the new name," from Accenture press release, 14 October 2000.

page 112: Kevin Keller's case study from Dartmouth's Tuck School of Business: Professor Kevin Keller and Keith Richey, *Accenture: Rebranding and Repositioning a Global Power Brand,* draft, 15 February 2002.

page 112: Kevin Keller's class questions from "Strategic Brand Management" course syllabus: www.dartmouth.edu/dart/chico/tuck_mba_program.syllabus?p_id=SBM.

page 114: "The Andersen name is likely to live on in the popular culture," from John A. Byrne, "Joe Berardino presided over the biggest accounting scandals ever," *BusinessWeek,* 12 August 2002.

page 114: "Andersen is now a very lame horse," from Kurt Eichenwald, "Enron's Many Strands: The Accountants; Miscues, Missteps, and the Fall of Andersen," *New York Times,* 8 May 2002.

6. Into the Vernacular

page 119: "by 2002, 27 percent of all servers . . . ran Linux," from Associated Press, 30 May 2002.

page 119: "computer code is akin to language," from Lawrence Lessig, *The Future of Ideas* (New York: Random House, 2001), 24.

page 120: "the necessity of owning a word," from Jean-Marie Dru, *Disruption: Overturning Conventions and Shaking Up the Marketplace* (New York: John Wiley & Sons, 1996), 99.

page 120: Interview with Gayle Christensen, 7 June 2001.

page 121: "classsic information theory," from Jerome S. Bruner, *Acts of Meaning: Four Lectures on Mind and Culture* (Cambridge: Harvard University Press, 1990), 5.

page 121: "Most products are bought verbally," from Al Ries, *Focus: The Future of Your Company Depends on It* (New York: HarperBusiness, 1997), 97.

page 122: "Dictionaries are, when you think," from Jack Hitt, *In a Word* (New York: Dell, 1992), 3.

page 123: "It is often claimed," from Preface to the Third Edition of the *OED,* www.oed.com/public/guide/preface_6.htm#distractions.

page 123: "Words, like individuals or nations," from Donald Hall and Sven Birkerts, *Writing Well,* 9th ed. (New York: Longman, 1998), 84.

page 123: "Synthetic words have bloomed," from J. C. Herz, "A Name So Smooth the Product Glides In," *New York Times,* 26 December 1998.

7. Love Is the Drug

page 125: "Put simply, the pop reference," from David Foster Wallace, "E Unibus Pluram: Television and U.S. Fiction," in *A Supposedly Fun Thing I'll Never Do Again: Essays and Arguments* (New York: Little, Brown, 1997), 42.

page 126: *"Depend Adult Undergarment,"* from David Foster Wallace, *Infinite Jest* (New York: Little, Brown, 1996).

page 126: "galloping across the Lucent Technologies Lawn," from Jonathan Franzen, *The Corrections* (New York: Farrar, Straus & Giroux, 2001), 36, 38.

page 127: "Ambien. Dexedrine," from Walter Kirn, *Up in the Air* (New York: Doubleday, 2001), 231.

page 128: David Wood speaking about Prozac quoted in Julie Erlich, "Giving Drugs a Good Name," *The New York Times Magazine,* 3 September 1995. (This article provides a good background on Wood Worldwide, as well.)

page 136: Specifics on drug naming from Linda Gundersen, "The Complex Process of Naming Drugs," *Annals of Internal Medicine* 129, no. 8, (15 October 1998).

page 136: A good deal of information about drug names in this chapter was gleaned from John W. Kenagy and Gary C. Stein, "Naming, Labeling, and Packaging of Pharmaceuticals," *American Journal of Health-System Pharmacists,* 58, no. 21 (2001):3033–34. © 2001 American Society of Health-System Pharmacists.

page 137: Rogaine history from Julie Erlich, "Giving Drugs a Good Name," *The New York Times Magazine,* 3 September 1995.

page 138: Background on Barr Labs from Amy Barrett, "Bruce Downey, Generic Drug Lord," *Business Week,* 1 October 2001.

page 138: The reverse-engineering and renaming of drugs was described in Donald G. McNeil Jr., "Selling Cheap 'Generic' Drugs, India's Copycats Irk Industry," *New York Times,* 1 December 2000.

page 142: "becoming a more or less direct path," from Thomas Frank, *One Market Under God* (New York: Doubleday, 2000), 294.

page 144: "a more powerful platform for consumer brand building," from Rebecca Robins and Tom Blackett, eds., *Brand Medicine: The Role of Branding in the Pharmaceutical Industry* (New York: Palgrave, 2001), 261.

page 144: Medical applications versus lifestyle applications, from Robins and Blackett, eds., *Brand Medicine,* 260.

page 145: FDA rating system from Marcel Corstjens and Marie Carpenter, "From Managing Pills to Managing Brands," *Harvard Business Review,* March–April 2000.

page 145: "Schering-Plough's Claritin," from Stephen S. Hall, "Prescription for Profit," *The New York Times Magazine,* 11 March 2001. This article helped to explain the success of the top-selling allergy drug Claritin, despite any great leaps in therapeutic effectiveness, and the article also painted an overall picture of the industry and the process of bringing a drug to market.

page 146: "It is important to remember that the brand name," from Robins and Blackett, eds., *Brand Medicine,* 161–62.

page 152: "165 million people worldwide take Pfizer medications" and $7.1 billion research figure from Gardiner Harris, "A Drug Giant Thinks It Can Grow Still Bigger," *New York Times*, 19 June 2003.

page 157: Viagra sales figures from Pfizer 2002 Annual Report and press releases.

page 157: Pfizer's work with Bob Dole from David Goetzl, "*Ad Age* Marketer of the Year: Pfizer. What Next After Viagra, Lipitor and Celebrex?," *Ad Age*, 10 December 2001.

page 158: List of user-endorsers from Robins and Blackett, eds., *Brand Medicine*, 289.

page 159: "In San Francisco," from Marilyn Chase, "A Doctor Fights for New Warnings on Viagra Labels," *Wall Street Journal*, 7 March 2003.

page 161: "I owe all of this turbulence and happiness to Viagra," from Philip Roth, *The Human Stain* (New York: Houghton Mifflin, 2000), 32.

page 162: Use of Viagra in China from Elisabeth Rosenthal, "An Age Old Quest Could Be at an End: Chinese Hail Viagra," *New York Times*, 23 April 2002.

page 163: Viagra in the *OED*, from *OED* online, New Edition, draft entry September 2001.

page 163: Stephen King, *On Writing* (New York: Scribner, 2000), 223.

While writing this book, I got a curious number of junk email messages that seemed to prove that certain words had become a part of the vernacular. The messages were simple. My favorite combined Budweiser's *Whassup!* message with Pfizer's, and FedEx's. It read:

Subject: Viagra, It's Whaazzz UP!
Sender: viagranow3661@yahoo.com
Viagra is the breakthrough medication that has restored or enhanced the Sex lives of millions of men . . . and women. Now available to you online and delivered via FedEx to your home or office at the lowest prices found anywhere.

Another one read poetically:

Improve Your Erections
Enhance Your Sexual Experience
Your Woman will Love You
Viagara [*sic*]

And another, not so poetically:

Subject: PARTY ALL NIGHT! VIAGRA ONLINE
BE A SUPERSTUD! VIAGRA ONLINE!
STAY HARD FOR HOURS, MAKE HER BEG FOR MORE!
BE THE TALK OF THE TOWN. BE A SEXUAL DYNAMO!

And another titled "ready when you are":

Fast acting viagra
Sonic15 is the actual Pfizer Viagra but works in under 15 minutes.
How does it work? Just place Sonic15 under your tongue and let it melt.
It will absorb directly into your system and bypass having to go through
the digestive system. Regular Viagra - 60 to 90 minutes Sonic15 - 5 to
15 minutes

8. Getting the Word Out

page 166: Background for the discussion of the Budweiser campaign
and Bob Lachky quotations come from Patricia Winters Lauro,
"Whassup? America's Asking," *New York Times,* 16 February 2001.

page 168. "Memes that deal with sex," from Susan Blackmore, *The
Meme Machine* (Oxford University Press, 1999), 121.

page 170: "Stadiums have been known . . . as long as thirty years," from
Scott Thurm, "Enron Is Latest to Suffer Jinx After Striking Stadium-
Naming Deal," *Wall Street Journal,* 4 December 2001.

page 170: A great deal of the background on the naming of Mile High
came through reading the extensive reporting of Cindy Brovsky of the
Denver Post.

page 175: Rick Reilly, "Corpo-Name Disease: Stop the Plague!," *Sports
Illustrated,* 9 January 2001.

page 176: "Excuse us," from Glenn Guzzo, "Editorial: Still a Mile
High," *Denver Post,* 8 August 2001.

page 178: "Culture Jammer's Manifesto" from Kalle Lasn's *Culture Jam:
The Uncooling of America* (New York: Eagle Brook, 1999), 128.

9. Stories

page 180: "We tell ourselves stories," from Joan Didion, *The White
Album* (New York: Simon & Schuster, 1979), 11.

page 180: Chip Heath's research into urban legends comes from Chip Heath, Chris Bell, and Emily Sternberg, "Emotional Selection in Memes: The Case of Urban Legends," *Journal of Personality and Social Psychology* 81: 1028–41.

page 181: Starbucks caffeine levels from Ron Rosenbaum, "Banned from Starbucks!," *New York Observer,* 14 June 1999.

page 182: Enron as the greatest story ever` told from Paul Krugman, "Death by Guru," *New York Times,* 18 December 2001.

page 183: The notion of culture, from Richard A. Barrett, *Culture and Conduct: An Excursion in Anthropology* (Belmont, Calif.: Wadsworth Publishing, 1984), 54; and John Seabrook, *No Brow: The Marketing of Culture—The Culture of Marketing* (New York: Vintage Books, 2001), 70.

page 184: "a focus group on wheels" and David Bostwick quotations from Ruth Shalit, "The Return of the Hidden Persuaders," *Salon.com,* 27 September 1999.

page 184: Interview with Dr. G. Clotaire Rapaille, 10 August 2001.

page 185: John P. Kotter and James L. Heskett, *Corporate Culture and Performance* (New York: Free Press, 1992), 4.

page 186: "The story then spreads as a coherent way of thinking," from interview with Chip Heath, Stanford University.

10. Futurecasting

page 187: The title for this chapter comes from Stone Yamashita Partners' self-published book, *Seismic Change*. It's a term they use to "examine the world your company is going to live in next month, next year, five or ten years from now." *Seismic Change,* no. 5.

page 187: "Whoever controls the language," from *Seismic Change,* no. 13.

page 188: Stone Yamashita Partners' self-published books: *Chemistry: And the Catalysts for Seismic Change,* © 2001 Stone Yamashita Partners; and *Seismic Change: A Manual for Agents of Change,* © 2000, Stone Yamashita Partners.

page 189: Debra Dunn, from an interview on 8 January 2002, and also quoted in Polly LaBarre, "Keith Yamashita Wants to Reinvent Your Company," *Fast Company Magazine,* November 2002.

page 191: Saturn background from David Aaker, *Building Strong Brands* (New York: The Free Press, 1996), 37–66.

page 193: "Sociologists have long recognized," from Dunbar, *Grooming, Gossip, and the Evolution of Language* (Cambridge: Harvard University Press, 1996), 205.

page 195: "How you tell the story determines who will listen," from *Seismic Change,* no. 7.

page 200: "We had to strike a balance," from Lou Gerstner, *Who Says Elephants Can't Dance* (New York: HarperBusiness, 2002), 173.

page 202: "When someone buys an Apple," from Bradley Johnson, "He Made the Best Ad Ever," *Wired,* August 1995.

page 203: "creative," from Randall Rothenberg, *Where the Suckers Moon: The Life and Death of an Advertising Campaign* (New York: Vintage Books, 1995), 10. This book traces the Subaru account as it is handled by Portland, Oregon's Wieden + Kennedy in the early 1990s. It is the best reported book I have read about advertising.

page 203: "Years later, Gerstner would say," from Steve Lohr, "He Likes to Win. At IBM, He Did," *New York Times,* 10 March 2002.

page 204: Gerstner on the "galvanizing mission," from Gerstner, *Who Says Elephants Can't Dance,* 213.

page 204: IBM's *One Voice,* © 1997 International Business Machines, 2–3, 47, 65.

page 208: "People carried it with them and read it like a bible . . . ," from "How Communications Helped Turn IBM Around," *Holmes Report,* 12 April 2001 (www.holmesreport.com/holmestemp/story.cfm?edit_id89 &typeid=2).

page 208: Iwata and *One Voice* from "How *One Voice* Has Changed IBM," by Jon Iwata in "Driving Corporate Culture: Aligning Your People, Your Business Strategy, and Your Brand," *Arthur W. Page Society Journal,* 26–28, 16th Annual Spring Seminar, 4–5 April 2001, New York City.

page 208: After reading dozens of books about branding, one tends to see mention of the same stories again and again. I came up with a quick test of these books, to gauge originality. The test included determining which of these following oft-cited stories were included: Nike, Starbucks, Coke (and the New Coke debacle), Volkswagen (the new Beetle), and Saturn. These cases often are mentioned because they offer a chance to see some of the best success stories. Whether or not they offer a way for other firms to incorporate best practices is more debatable. They are often armchair adventures for marketing readers. And the people who are affiliated with these successes are often the people writing about them. As for *Chemistry,* I found that the folks at Stone Yamashita had included a rather long study of Coke, many brief mentions of Nike, no mentions of Starbucks, and a few medium-size mentions of Saturn.

page 211: "We both knew that IBM was better served," from *Chemistry,* 2002–5.

page 211: Lou Gerstner exit interview comments quoted in Lohr, "He Likes to Win," *New York Times,* 10 March 2002.

page 212: "We'd challenge them to set a BHAG," from Jerry I. Porras and James C. Collins, *Built to Last: Successful Habits of Visionary Companies* (New York: Harper Business, 1994), 224.

page 212: "challenge them to ask every employee . . . ," from Porras and Collins, *Built to Last,* 225.

page 213: "Every aspect of the company has been reassessed," from Jean-Marie Dru, *Disruption: Overturning Conventions and Shaking Up the Marketplace* (New York: John Wiley & Sons, 1996), 97.

page 213: "brand environmentalists," from Scott Bedbury, *A New Brand World* (New York: Viking, 2002), 131.

page 213: "pronounced IBM irrelevant," from John Markoff, "The IBM Era Is Over," *New York Times,* 16 December 1992.

page 213: "The revival of IBM over the last nine years," from Lohr, "He Likes to Win."

page 214: "helped establish IBM as the leader," from Gerstner, *Who Says Elephants Can't Dance,* 92.

ACKNOWLEDGMENTS

A book like this can be written only with the input of people in the field—and I am grateful to all those who shared their work with me: David Placek, Marc Hershon, and Steve Price of Lexicon; Dave Werezak of Research In Motion; Hugh Dubberly of Dubberly Design; namers Andrea Michaels and Andrew Chaikin; David Wood and R. John Fidelino of InterbrandWood Healthcare; Jim Murphy, Teresa Poggenpohl, and Darienne Dennis of Accenture; and Laura Keeton at IBM. Keith Yamashita patiently answered my many questions, as did his colleagues Allison Koch and Lisa Maulhardt. Professor Chip Heath at Stanford's Graduate School of Business listened to my thoughts about idea transfer while offering larger lessons. For ideas and contacts I owe thanks to Cindy Brovsky of the *Denver Post,* Lili Weigert, Joseph Groth, and Jon Steel. A few people talked with me confidentially—I appreciate their help.

Several friends and family members read and commented extensively on the manuscript at various key points; thanks go out to Michael Megalli (and the team at Group 1066), Glasgow Phillips, and Elizabeth Gould. Jessie Scanlon has long provided valuable editorial insights and support. I owe thanks to Pete Leyden, who edited an original article about naming at *Wired,* and to Kit Combes at *The New York Times Magazine.* For participation in our experiment in naming, I owe thanks to Aaron Gigliotti (who joined the company in its later stages), to Matt Rolandson, Beth O'Rourke, Susan Gould, Margaret Partlow, Ted Paff, and our many clients. Thanks go out to my friend Steve "idea guy" Cassel, for the many whiteboard sessions. Steve and our officemates Brian West and Josh McHugh offered just enough distraction and support along the way. I appreciate the help of Peter Barnes and the Mesa Refuge; Abby Weintraub; young adman Richard Bronshvag; my parents, Chuck and Diane Frankel; the indefatigable Uma; and Peter Waldman's invaluable double assist. I am obliged to Bernard Burk and Simon Frankel for their timely legal counsel, and to my brother Matt for coming through with critical medical information. In the preparation of this book I am indebted to Michelle Jeffers for research assistance. She gets my *Google* award for her rare ability to track down arcane facts. And to Emily McManus, who proved a solid reader and editor of the book in its formative stages.

Writing this book, from start to finish, was made immeasurably easier through the aid of my good friend Tucker Nichols. He brought great understanding and interest to the project and offered reams of sage advice. My agent, Bonnie Nadell, was a fan of the book from the time our paths crossed. I owe my gratitude to both Bonnie and her colleague Irene Moore. I am grateful to publisher Steve Ross and the staff at Crown, who pitched in with their enthusiasm and ideas for the book—especially Tara Gilbride, Melanie Denardo, Mario Rojas, and my editor, Annik La Farge, who steered with a strong vision and pushed the book in the right direction with grace.

INDEX

P

PageWriter, 53
Palm Computing, 10, 66, 74, 191
Palmeiro, Rafael, 158
Palm vs. palm, 66–67
patent laws, 106, 138–39
Paxil, 136
Pei, I. M., 171
Pentium chip, 50, 54, 59–60, 64, 75
Petersen, Kim, 108–10
Pfizer, 130, 152–64
pharmaceutical industry, 127–64
    advertising in, 135, 141, 145–47
    brand awareness in, 127–28, 145–47
    control exercised in, 150
    cost of new drugs in, 135–36, 144
    drug names in, 136–37
    drug patents in, 135–36, 138
    forecasts in, 139–43
    lifestyle drugs in, 143–47
    naming process in, 140–41
    placebo effect in, 162–63
    registered trademarks in, 144
    regulatory obstacles in, 134, 135–39
    target markets in, 147–51
    trade dress in, 138, 156–57
    Viagra, 152–64
    and Wood Worldwide, 127–31, 147–49
Pharmacia, 131
Philip Morris, 81–82, 98–99
Phillips, Glasgow, 26–34, 132–34, 160
Pilot Pens, 67
Pitney Bowes, 61
placeholder names, 62
Placek, David, 46–51, 54–62, 80
    and BlackBerry, 54, 59, 62, 64, 69, 70–71
    and divergent thinking, 48, 55–57, 58, 75
PocketLink, 53–54, 59–61, 62, 76

Poggenpohl, Teresa, 91–94, 95, 112, 113
Pollan, Tom, 92
Pontiac Aztek, 43
Porras, James, 212
Porsche:
    Boxster, 35, 36, 40
    Carrera, 36, 38
    Cayenne, 8, 9, 12, 35–42, 45, 215–16
    model 911, 35, 40, 41–43
    PR strategy of, 41
    Targa, 36
Porsche Cars of North America, 41
PowerBook, 46, 49–50, 64, 65
Price, Steve, 46, 47, 48, 56–58, 63
Prilosec, 137, 157
problem solving, 56–57
Procter & Gamble, 67–68
products, experience with, 79–80
Prozac, 124, 128, 129–30, 131, 133, 138, 163
Public Broadcasting System (PBS), 194–95
PwC Consulting, 115, 194

Q

Quiddity, 27–34, 132–34

R

Rand, Paul, 196
RAND Corporation, 55
Rapaille, G. Clotaire, 184–85
Redhill, David, 103–4
reengineering, 86
Reilly, Rick, 175
Relpax, 159–60
Rich Foods, 170
Ries, Al, 96, 110, 121–22
RIM (Research In Motion), 59–68
    and PocketLink, 52–54
    and product expansion, 76
    see also BlackBerry
Riney, Hal & Partners, 191, 192
Rosenbaum, Ron, 181
Rothenberg, Randall, 203

ABOUT THE
AUTHOR

Alex Frankel has written the "On Language" column for *The New York Times Magazine* and reported on business culture for *Wired, Fast Company,* and *Outside.* His interest in synthetic language led him to launch his own naming firm and spend twelve months hunting down the origins of leading brand names. He lives within shouting distance of the Golden Gate Bridge.